SMILING THROUGH STUMBLING BLOCKS

Sonny O. Braide

ISBN 978-1-956001-77-8 (paperback)
ISBN 978-1-956001-78-5 (eBook)

Copyright © 2021 by Sonny O. Braide

All rights reserved. No part of this publication may be reproduced, distributed, or transmitted in any form or by any means, including photocopying, recording, or other electronic or mechanical methods without the prior written permission of the publisher.

Printed in the United States of America

CONTENTS

Dedication v
Forward vii
The Author xi
Introduction xiii
Block Number 1 – Lost Father soon after birth 1
Block Number 2 – Primary School stalled 4
Block Number 3 – Attempt hatched to sabotage CD's Lagos prospect 7
Block Number 4 – No money for transport fare 9
Block Number 5 – Took a job of dead-ended movement 11
Block Number 6 – CD advised against taking shorthand courses! ... 16
Block Number 7 – FTC opportunity denied 19
Block Number 8 – Upward movement tied to exam success 22
Block Number 9 – Discriminatory laws in the Civil Service 25
Block Number 10 – Music as alternative? 28
Block Number 11 – Apartheid in the country's Foreign Service 35
Block Number 12 – Transfer application got missing in the FPSC ... 39
Block Number 13 – Beast of burden 41
Block Number 14 – Dearth of vacancies 49
Block Number 15 – No overseas posting for CD 51
Block Number 16 – Tertiary Education Impeded 53

Block Number 17 – Certificate evaluation stalled! 56
Block Number 18 – No more age exemptions for NYSC.................58
Block Number 19 – NYSC deprived CD of conversion....................60
Block Number 20 – Conversion grade level reversed down!.............62
Block Number 21 – Conversion tied to academy attendance............64
Block Number 22 – Pensions stumbling blocks 69
Block Number 23 – No more job opportunities for CD..................74
Block Number 24 – Wasteful training to become a Vehicle-
                   Salesman...76
Irony of fate vs Success Story 79
Stumbling Blocks - Blessings in disguise 89
The lesson learned..91
The road to Success..93
Be grateful to God in all circumstances..95
Acknowlegement..99
Quotations used in this book 101
Other Book Titles by The Author...105

DEDICATION

This book is dedicated to:

1. My mother who gave me life full of love;
2. My forever better-half – Queenba – who had been multi-tasking very efficiently and effectively as Mother, Sister, Friend, Lover, and Wife; without whom this book will not even be thought of, let alone written and published;
3. All those our children who, not only call me father; but also gave me and their mother love, and up-to-date upkeep to enable us remain alive and well-fed.
4. My ever-present Cousin and Father-figure, Bishop A. N. C. Iyalla, JP, an equally accomplished Godly man who has stood strongly to support and guide in my fight through this earthly stumbling blocks; and
5. To my known and unknown adversaries, for making me stronger by driving all the wedges enumerated in this book, between me and progress.

FORWARD

> If there's a book you really want to read,
> but it hasn't been written yet,
> then you must write it.
> *-Toni Morrison*

"6 Stumbling Blocks," written by a Nigerian-born, has come at the appropriate time when honesty and hard work is now at its lowest ebb in today's society, especially among the youths. Nobody wants to work hard with honesty and perseverance for a living. Of course, some, if not most of them imbibe this abhorrent character from some of their older generation whom Satan manipulated to acquire the "get-rich-quick" syndrome without working for it. They want what they do not have, so they kill to get it. They long for what others have, and cannot afford it, so they start a fight to take it away from them.

They have forgotten that when the first human pair in the Christian Bible, Adam and Eve disobeyed God, the Almighty decreed unto man that:

> "----cursed is the ground for your sake. In sorrow shall you eat of it all the days of your life. Thorns also and thistles shall it bring forth unto you--- In the sweat of your face shall you eat bread till you return unto the ground --" *-Gen. 3: 17-19.*

Thus, it is clear that man has to work laboriously and assiduously for a living; and while working hard, oppositions, discouragements and set-backs are bound to be there. That is the Biblical "thorns and thistles" which the author has described here as "stumbling blocks". But the secret of success in life is based on honesty, perseverance and contentment. This is in consonance with what my late uncle (a widely experienced mentor of mine who spent over twenty-four years in Europe and America) had taught me at the age of twelve, that "Nothing great or good can be accomplished without labor and toil. This has been my motto in life.

I know the author, Mr. Sonny Oko Braide from his formative years. Being born also without silver spoon in his mouth, but through dint of hard work amidst myriads of obstacles, he waded through to get some enviable achievements. He took so much interest on the life of his portrayed CD, who exhibited similar trait of obstinate courage and found the veritable golden needle in a haystack.

As pointed out by the author, this is a true story, and so the book should not be regarded as a fictitious autobiographic narrative. It should rather be seen as challenges in life and how to overcome them with determination. I therefore, recommend this book, not only to youths to emulate the character's life, but also to young adults who are yet to see the light of successful life in the other end of the tunnel.

Based on the foundation of honesty, sincerity and the fear of God, rewards are for those who are prepared to work hard, make sacrifices and oppose set-backs with determination, courage and endurance. That is what this book is all about. If youths and young adults can inculcate in them the above morals, illegal and unworthy acts such as examination malpractices, corruption in low and high places, as well as all criminal activities will be eliminated, and the world will be a blessed, better place.

To the matured minds, however, the book has a tint of entertainment and an insight to the goings-on in the portrayed country's Diplomatic Service. Above all, the book is philosophical and highly inspirational.

Parents, guardians, head teachers, school principals, and the general reading public are therefore urged to have "Stumbling Blocks," individually as a must for the home and library.

Bishop A. N. C. Iyalla, JP
St. Jude's Cathedral
Christ Army Church
49/50 Creek Road
Port Harcourt, Rivers State, NIGERIA.

THE AUTHOR

Sonny Braide – a very prominent son of the Kalabari Nation, has earlier successfully produced and published three interesting hot-selling books, before embarking on this very apt publication.

He was born (1942) in Bakana, Kalabari, Rivers State of Nigeria; and had made writing his hobby.

He was a musician, and a diplomat; and now a Writer.

Mr. Braide lives in El Paso, Texas with his family.

INTRODUCTION

> The fairest graciousness, they say, is a
> kindly look. Wherever it thrives,
> the whole world flourishes.
> - *Hindu Wisdom*

This book – "Stumbling Blocks" - epitomizes the struggle of man in his sojourn on earth. It is a true story of a very close hard-working friend, who goes by his initials – CD. The name was so famous in his domain that some call him Sidi while many others just use it as initial "C.D." One remarkable major characteristic of this man is his ever-smiling countenance. Many around CD, deceived by his ever-pleasant visage, continued to nurture the erroneous belief that he had never had any problems in life, hence he could afford to smile the way he did. Some even resorted to branding him as fool, for smiling even in situations that ought to be taken seriously.

What these other people failed to realize is that, like all humans on this earth, CD's life had been full of stumbling blocks; but he had the fortitude to handle those within his powers, and leave the rest to God who only knows why things happen to human-beings. But to give some credit to those who think smiling must be confined to only those times when situations are comfortable, I began to embark on research to find out the goodness, if any, of smiling; and the answers confirmed positively; hence the decision to bring this story to all those who care that smiling under all situations is not misplaced after all; and stumbling blocks are indeed a ***blessing in disguise.***

Having faced so many stumbling blocks personally in life, I thought I had gone through too much; but considering CD's life, I found that mine pales tremendously in comparison. My experience, coupled with the teachings I had undertaken in the journey through life, had confirmed to me that troubles are actually our steppingstones if only we recognize them as such and take the right steps. To confirm this conviction, we need to learn from no other lesser creatures than a donkey as narrated in this legendary farmer's story.

> "A farmer's donkey fell into a well, and cried piteously for hours while the farmer tried to figure out what to do. With no hope of success in sight, the owner finally decided that the animal was old anyway, and the well needed to be covered up after all; so, it just wasn't worth it to retrieve the donkey. He invited his neighbors to help him cover the well, and they all grabbed a shovel each and began to shovel dirt into the well. At first, the donkey realized what was happening and cried horribly; but then, to everyone's amazement the animal quieted down!
>
> A few shovel-loads later, the farmer finally looked down the well and was astonished at what he saw. Apparently, with each shovel of dirt that hit its back, the donkey was doing something amazing; shaking the dirt off and taking a step up. The more shovels of dirt were dumped on its back, the quicker the donkey would shake them off and elevate itself up.

Finally, the donkey stepped up over the edge of the well and happily trotted off, to everyone's amazement."

That is a good lesson for we humans, who have the faculties to contemplate and make decisions for ourselves in this world of challenges. But regrettably, smiling has been an asset that eludes a great number of people. We had severally encountered ridicules by people who thought they were wiser to know when not to smile! But ever before I heard that it takes a frightening number of 65 muscles to frown, but only 15 to smile, I personally, like CD, had been smiling; convinced that there must be appreciable benefits to be in that mood at all times. Truly, successes of our life stories have confirmed that smiling through stumbling blocks does indeed yield profitable results in the end. That is why I thought of bringing out this story to inspire all people, young and old, not to despair, but smile through your life's never-ending stumbling blocks.

For this reason, it is worth reading and learning from the following many stumbling blocks that my ever-smiling friend, CD encountered and overcame in life.

BLOCK NUMBER 1

LOST FATHER SOON AFTER BIRTH

Soon after CD was born (a fourth child of his mother) his father, a well-to-do businessman, died. Notably, at the time the father married CD's mother, he was already advanced in age; but his tribal custom did not object to older men getting married to younger women, some of whom as young as their grand-daughters. However, this man did not die of old age, but of frustration and depression when it was discovered to his chagrin that his own first son from earlier marriage, had been branded a witch.

CD's father, at his death, was survived by his five children and two wives - his mother and an older woman who was childless. Unfortunately, this older woman was living with him when he died, and so, it was she, and his estranged son from an earlier marriage that inherited nearly all his properties.

Thus, having been deprived of any inheritance whatsoever from his father, CD and his sisters lacked adequate provision for upkeep and education. Their well-to-do father's estate was "looted" and usurped by the combined callous and selfish son; live-in older wife; and the greater family relations who shared among themselves all his belongings, with virtually no consideration whatsoever for his young children. Thus, being deprived of any inheritance, and lack of assistance, none of CD's older sisters was shown the road to school as their poor mother could not afford. However, When CD grew up to school age, their mother vowed that the boy must go to school, no matter what. In this regard, she was encouraged by CD's paternal uncle, who just returned from the United States, and was managing a paint production business. He could not offer her any financial help though, but gave her concession to pluck the fruits from the coconut trees planted by CD's father at the adjacent waterside for sale, to pay for the boy's school fees.

But at her very first attempt to reach one coconut tree, the uncle's younger sisters (who were both older than her) confronted her, and warned her never to go any closer to any fruit tree within their territory. They wondered why she would all of a sudden decide to pluck fruits of the trees that had been inherited by them! All explanations that it was their elder brother who gave her permission, fell on deaf ears, and they even did not want to wait for their big brother to verify her story. Being a peace-loving woman, CD's mother just walked away, seeing their determined resolve to deprive her of that which in reality belonged to her late husband.

Nevertheless, with stout determination, CD's poor mother stubbornly went pass this block number one, and saw him through primary education. The boy would have remained behind the local township, like most of his colleagues then, and ended up as a fisherman. But that was not the case for this enterprising young boy who seemed to have a mission; and for that, all was not lost. Luck shone on him after primary education, and for some miraculous circumstances, he was picked up by a budding local philanthropist, to get paid employment in the country's capital city.

Very new to the world, CD was totally oblivious of the first series of stumbling blocks that confronted him right at birth. After all, his single mother rose to the occasion to bring him up as best as she could. So, innocently, **CD kept on smiling**. After all, as Lou Holtz stated:

> Life is ten percent what happens to you,
> and ninety percent how you respond to it.
> *- Lou Holtz*

BLOCK NUMBER 2

PRIMARY SCHOOL STALLED

Wait a minute! It is worthwhile to note that built-in within Block Number one was Block Number 2 which was also overcome. Since female education was not equally encouraged at the time, CD's mother did not care very much that her earlier three daughters did not attend school. But when my friend grew up to school age, the mother determined that he being the only boy at that time, must attend school; and so, went ahead to register him in school. But then, Block **Number 2** showed up!

The second strike happened when CD got to what was known as Primary II. His mother got pregnant with his younger brother; and to prepare for the boy's coming, she was left with no option than to withdraw my friend from school temporarily. During this pregnancy, she allowed her male cousin to take CD to the Cameroon (where he was doing fishing as a trade)! Ignorant of what he was going into, CD got excited at the prospect to leave town with a beloved elder cousin who was popularly called "Uncle".

However, just as CD was beginning to get used to the fisherman's life barely after a year, his mother began sending series of messages, asking for CD's return; having taken care of his new-born brother's immediate child-birth needs. After several months, and sensing that her messages were being ignored, she mandated the leader of a Church delegation on mission to the town's community in the fishing villages in the Cameroun's, to bring the boy with him. With the physical presence of such an eminent personality, her cousin had no choice but to let CD go.

My friend thus returned to school, and still maintaining his brilliancy, he was given double promotion within one year. As an A+ student, CD was always the first on the promotion list from "Infant 1" through to "Standard VI." But then, just as he was cruising to the finish line, Block Number 2 stock again in form of lack of fund. The boy could not be readmitted into his last term (semester) because his previous term fee was still pending unpaid. With no help from anywhere, his mother tried to appease him with promises to let him repeat classes the following year at another town, with extended family members. But CD lost hope completely; querying the feasibility of completing in another town, and among total unfamiliar relations with more expenses, what he could not do at home.

However, just as CD and his mother were working on the prospect to continue his last term classes the following year, **Block Number 2** got cleared. The Headmaster of his school sent for the boy to come back to school for the final exams, as he had achieved required number of attendances! The school was just beginning to recover from poor results, and would not want to jeopardize its record should such a potential success student as CD, was denied the opportunity to take the final regional examination.

The plan was to withhold the boy's certificate should he succeed, until all his outstanding school fees were cleared. CD gladly went back to school; sat the First School Leaving Examination at the due time; and when the result came out, CD PASSED! Out of 26 students only 17 passed; making his group the pioneers of good results at an era that lasted six years when many primary schools of the entire Region, were for some inexplicable reasons, scoring zero results. CD thus finally made it through **Block Number 2** and remained smiling.

If the Moon is your friend,
you'll never work in darkness
-*Ghanaian Saying*

BLOCK NUMBER 3

ATTEMPT HATCHED TO SABOTAGE CD'S LAGOS PROSPECT

After graduating from primary school with no move forward in sight, a budding local philanthropist appeared from seemingly nowhere by Divine intervention, with an offer to take CD to the country's capital city. The story sounded quite unbelievable to CD's mother until she heard the offer direct from the great personality visiting home on vacation. The poor woman thanked him profusely with invocation of God's blessing as she left with her son.

On his return to the city and while negotiating for my friend's job, a cousin of CD's approached the philanthropist's bosom friend at home with a fabricated lie that my CD was boasting about town of his imminent capital city prospect. This was very damaging because the philanthropist warned CD to make the offer a great secret, as there were so many other relations begging him for such help, and theirs were put off.

This man was about sending the surprise message to his friend in the city to forget CD's matter, but God intervened; putting it in his mind to first get CD's version of the story before taking action. The man did accordingly; summoning CD to see him urgently. When confronted with the query, by mentioning the name of the guy who told him the story, my friend was shocked and very angry to hear such lies about him by his very close cousin. He denied vehemently and asked the man to summon the story-teller to face him with the facts.

On the appointed date and time CD arrived at the elder's home and found his close cousin sitting relaxed without knowing why he was there. After the usual pleasantries, the elder "took the opportunity" of CD's presence to pop the question of why CD was propagating his city prospect in gross disobedience of the injunction placed on him against that! When CD categorically denied the allegation, the elder then turned to CD's cousin, who incidentally was also related to the elder, to mention any single person outside the family cycle who had ever learned of CD's city story.

The lying cousin was greatly embarrassed, as he could not substantiate his story. The elder then rebuked him from any such action that could foment discord within the family. The elder then turned to plead with CD to forgive his cousin who acted innocently. That was how attempts to thwart CD's Lagos prospect by **Block No. 3** failed; and CD moved on smiling, because he believed Frank A. Clark's saying that:

> If you find a path with no obstacles,
> it probably doesn't lead anywhere.
> *-Frank A. Clark*

BLOCK NUMBER 4

NO MONEY FOR TRANSPORT FARE

Eventually as promised, word came for CD to travel to the city, but alas, no transportation money for my friend! His mother was away to the fishing port close-by, so CD borrowed a boat and travelled there with his junior brother to inform their mother about the call; and asked for money to travel. Helpless, the mother accompanied them back home and began looking for where to borrow the amount which was hard to come by.

At that time, the country had a passenger ship named *"Ajasa"* that plied between his state capital and the country's headquarters; yet his mother found it hard to raise the minimal amount. To worsen situation, his mother's untie intervened very harshly; advising her not to bother struggling to borrow money because she did not believe that CD was actually going to Lagos. Her reason was that the boy just wanted that money for his adolescent squandering, as young people of those days did! CD was so mad with that grand-aunt's mischievous advice that he could not forget her uncalled-for interjection till she passed on.

However, as usual, the Almighty intervened, and another male elder relation stepped in with the required amount for CD's mother to pay her son to the city to begin a new life. Being an advocate of children leaving home to work for their future, this elder advised CD's mother to disregard her auntie's advice; assuring her that he knew CD very well as a responsible young man with great prospect. Thus, **Block No. 4** failed to stop CD from going to the city, and the young man remained smiling as usual, believing what James Rogers said that:

> Over every mountain there is a path,
> although it may not be seen from the valley.
> -James Rogers

BLOCK NUMBER 5

TOOK A JOB OF DEAD-ENDED MOVEMENT

My friend eventually arrived in the city where most of the stumbling blocks played themselves out for him. On arrival there, CD was first employed as a Fisherman in the Federal Fisheries Department. That was what his poor educational (Elementary Six Certificate) qualification could get him. The job was in the category of "General Labor" involving all kinds of cleaning, scrubbing, sweeping, cutting and carrying light and heavy stuff; as well as going out to sea to actually catch fish in a trawler boat! He had no choice, but to endure this humbling job. Humbling because the very trade he thought he had escaped from home – fishing – was what he ended up doing in the city, though in a modern way! But because he was determined not to let his mother down back home, he hoped for the best, and did not rest on his oars, as how to improve himself became his obsession.

The same Divine intervention happened soon again, to get him out of that job, as Federal Fishery Department was asked to relocate to a new site. It was the time of the country's fast-approaching Independence Day, and the government badly needed the site to build a five-star hotel to accommodate world leaders.

However, the site the office moved to was, at that time, in an uncharted and isolated area. Incidentally, there was also at the same time, the need to downsize the department's work force; and being among the latest employees, CD was among the few that were targeted for firing. However, the gentleman who took him to the city intervened with a friend at the personnel department to spare CD the agony of losing the job. So, this officer revised the decision as it affected CD and another boy named Lawrence, from his clan who he personally recruited; giving them a "temporary" position as Security Guards! The officer told CD's sponsor that the boy would keep watch at the facility from 2 o'clock in the afternoon at the close of office till 10 o'clock in the night when Lawrence would relieve him and work till dawn. Having no choice, CD accepted the offer.

But to CD's consternation, when the day came and he called for work in the afternoon, CD saw his friend Lawrence already there for work also. On inquiry, the friend told CD that the schedule had been changed for CD to work the night shift instead! Needless to say, CD got so disappointed and angry that he just walked away for good, with no attempt to confirm Lawrence's story.

The next day CD called on his sponsor to inform him of the favoritism the officer at the establishment played against him, by asking CD to do a night shift at such a remote place; but to my friend's utmost disappointment, this sponsor encouraged him to still take up that job pending when he would find him another opening elsewhere. As CD could not argue with him, he just nodded and left, but refused to go back to the job of a night-guard. So angry, CD couldn't imagine himself just raw from his mother's protection in a local setting, to be a security guard in a wild unprotected remote area of a big city!

Understandably, to say the least, the sponsor was also very disappointed when his friend told him that CD had refused to report for duties; and not happy with the way CD handled the matter by not going back to him about his refusal of the offer, he took his hands off all of CD's affairs; maybe to see how this boy could survive without him.

But thank God, CD managed to subsist by joining an orchestra to play music at night clubs. In fact, the pay he got from music was even higher than his government minimum wage he was receiving.

Finally, a family man's intervention on CD's behalf yielded a positive result, and the sponsor secured a Janitor's job for the young man at the Federal Ministry of Education. Though not good enough for him, CD nevertheless took the job; regarding it as a stepping-stone that would keep him going until he would find a better one. The young man was determined to really move above that class in due course.

Luckily, it was the independence era, and efforts were being intensified to replace all colonial civil servants in government offices with indigenous citizens. But to achieve such position, one needed to be equipped with requisite qualifications.

The immediate trade that CD felt he could embark on under that situation, was typing; and he enrolled in commercial school; got trained to be a Typist – one of the few after-office-hours training facility available at the time. In those days, there was neither computer nor electric typewriter. People had to make do with manual typewriters which posed real hardship passing speed tests, as in many cases, the machines were old with rusty keyboards which would jam while on speed test. Moreover, the examinations came from Pitman's College, London twice a year. That situation forced students to be enrolling for two or three exams in advance in order not to wait too long in case one would not make the paper just taken. In spite of these problems, CD passed the official qualifying test at 25-words-per-minute to make Typist Grade III (3) position. Then, lack of vacancy prevented the boy from being converted; forcing him to hang on until when he was able to pass the test at 35-words-per-minute before getting converted to the post of a Grade II (2) Copy-Typist.

That was an improvement for him, both in status and take-home pay; but on getting there, CD discovered that the future prospect of this job was very limited. By regulation, when appointed to the post of Copy-Typist Grade III (3) after passing 25 words per minute (wpm), one would stay as long as it takes one to pass 35 wpm, to be upgraded Grade II (2). The same applied for upward movement to Grade One (I) (50 wpm). Yet after all is said and done, one stagnates on Salary Grade F3 forever! So, after getting his 50 words per minute typing certificate, and marking time on that grade for years, CD was advised to indulge fully into the secretarial line by studying shorthand writing to advance to the stenographer cadre.

That became a great challenge to CD; for after battling through with typing, how could he start all over again by venturing into shorthand writing? CD being the kind of person that likes to face challenges, he made up his die-hard determination to face the challenge head-on. It was a very bold attempt for my friend, as I recall having two other close friends who could hardly move beyond the beginning speed of 25 wpm in typewriting throughout their carrier. The first tried two times without making the result and decided to abandon any further try, while the second could not even remember that he had an exam to attend when the day arrived! They both just retired on that low level in abject poverty.

But for CD at that point in time, it was relatively easier as all that was needed was only to pass shorthand and typewriting at the required levels (80 wpm shorthand, and 35 wpm typewriting), to be called a Stenographer Grade III (3) which is the starting point for that cadre. Many young men and women successfully jumped the hurdle and were the envy of all in CD's shoes. By then, typing was no longer his problem, because he had already achieved the 50 wpm, which was more than the required entry speed. All he needed was to pass shorthand at

80 wpm. But that constituted his ***stumbling block number 5,*** because stenography (shorthand) posed a very difficult subject to learn, and to pass its examination.

> Obstacles don't have to stop you.
> If you run into a wall, don't turn around and give up.
> Figure out how to climb it, go through it, or work around it.
> *-Michael Jordan*

BLOCK NUMBER 6

CD ADVISED AGAINST TAKING SHORTHAND COURSES!

Since shorthand writing was the only way available to him, CD consulted an elder friend of his for advice on how to embark on it. This friend had taken courses in shorthand writing, sponsored by the government in search of high school graduates to fill the huge vacancy positions left open by the colonialist civil servants. But to his huge shock, this friend advised CD not to ever think of short-hand writing, because he (CD) did not have enough knowledge of English language needed to write shorthand!

CD was very disappointed to hear such a distracting advice from a trusted elder friend, but he refused to be deterred; and registered himself into a private secretarial school to learn shorthand writing. That was a daunting task because what he really lacked at that time, was time itself. He was working two jobs full-time – (1) day job in the office, and (2) night job, playing music at night-clubs. He had very few hours to sleep, yet my friend was satisfied with just few hours nap after work, and early hours of the day before venturing out to outsmart "Pick-pockets" while struggling for seats in scarce municipal bus for his office job.

Moreover, shorthand – a totally strange way of making certain strokes with pen and doing that as someone speaks or reads from a book was a daunting task. Furthermore, as his elder friend warned him, one has to know the English Language very well to be able to make sense of the words and sentences read out for one to transcribe them correctly. In other words, one was required to take English courses to know, for example, the difference from words like "sweet" from "suite" as the speaker calls them out in the context of the subject matter. So, in order to be vast in the English Language, CD was introduced to a book titled "The Seven Hundred English Common Words," published by an earlier British shorthand writer to be able to make headway.

Despite all that, CD scaled through, and passed shorthand writing within short space of time, at the required 80 wpm speed. It goes without saying that the young man was already over-qualified for the post of *Stenographer Grade III (3)*. But wait; **Block Number 6** was already there! A new government circular had been issued, embellished with some official verbiages:

> "The dearth of secretarial staff having been a thing of the past, there is no longer need to recruit this category of officers with only typing and shorthand knowledge. Therefore, to now qualify for secretarial job, a candidate must have three more additional subjects, namely: (1) English Language; (2) Office Routine; and (3) Secretarial Practice."

At that time, these additional courses could only be acquired by going to recognized commercial schools that offered them; and these schools were more or less non-existent in the country. That was what forced government agencies to sponsor people to undergo the secretarial courses at Pitman's College in London. Since it appeared that CD stood no chance of passing through this block, he thought he just had to remain a "Copy-typist" (as it was generally called) for life with no upward movement. Yet CD remained smiling.

However, so determined to write shorthand, CD had to do it privately, and finally, after a few months, was able to pass 80 words per minute (wpm) in Shorthand-writing-Examination conducted by the Royal Society of Arts (RSA) from London. Having that encouragement, he continued writing until he got 100 wpm; and 120 wpm respectively in quick succession in shorthand writing.

This proves a Chinese proverb that says: "The person who says it cannot be done should not interrupt the person who is doing it." The lesson learnt here, as confirmed by Picabo Street is:

> When someone tells me there is only one way to do things,
> it always lights a fire under my butt. My instant reaction is,
> "I'm going to prove you wrong!"
> -*Picabo Street*

BLOCK NUMBER 7

FTC OPPORTUNITY DENIED

CD programmed his mind to read for these subjects whenever the opportunity presented itself for one to get admission into the only institution then that offered the courses – the Federal Training Centre (FTC) – a government institution that was overseen by the Ministry of Establishments. But the realization of this hope was like the camel passing through the eye of the needle; because gaining admission into this school constituted **Block Number Seven 7.** To begin with, the school admitted only candidates who already had West African School Certificate (WASC) or General Certificate of Education (GCE) - (High School Certificate or GED); not Elementary Certificate that CD had at that time. However, luckily as he envisaged, after smiling for some years behind this block, there appeared a light at the end of the tunnel.

Faced with difficulties in attracting high school graduates to be trained as confidential secretaries, FTC authorities at long last agreed to accept candidates with Elementary School Certificate, but with some snags attached. These were that due to the short duration of the course

(18 months) such candidates must have already got some diplomas in shorthand (50/60 wpm) and typewriting (25 wpm), to train as stenographers. CD jumped for joy, as the requirements were below what he had already obtained. His boss was too eager to recommend him for the course, and when the call eventually came, CD was accepted with a few others in their Ministry (Education).

But this block just refused to give way. Slots were allocated to all government Ministries and Departments, and CD was surely among others in his Ministry to fill its allocated spots; but an aged Executive Officer in the Ministry's Open Registry where letters were received, processed and passed on for action, for some inexplicable reasons, misplaced the Admission Letter! Since all the affected people were very eagerly waiting for the call, they became very disappointed on learning that the course had already begun without them. It was their outcry that triggered an investigation as to why the Ministry was not represented, and the answer from the Ministry of Establishment revealed that the Education's invitation letters were sent out at the same time with those of others; and it was signed for. Internal investigation then revealed that the aged Executive Officer in charge at the Open Registry misplaced that important package containing the invitation message for about four people in the Ministry that included CD.

For depriving the Ministry of its quota, and thus denying its chosen candidates the great opportunity to improve their lot in life, the officer was severely reprimanded and caused to lose one year's salary raise. That, of course, was too late for CD, as the damage could not be undone. Yet my friend continued to remain positive and smiling.

It is better to be prepared for an
opportunity and not have one
than to have an opportunity
and not be prepared.
- *Whitney Young, Jr.*

BLOCK NUMBER 8

UPWARD MOVEMENT TIED TO EXAM SUCCESS

When the circular letter came the following year from the Establishment Ministry, all those affected in CD's Ministry could not wait for their Registry to pass anything to the schedule officer. They made sure that the officer saw the Admission Letter first before the Registry did. As soon as words filtered to them that the circular was out, they went to the issuing office at the Ministry of Establishment direct and got the one for the Ministry of Education. Again, the recommendation letter was also hand-carried by the affected staffers to the Establishment Ministry, with words left behind with the issuing section to please allow them to come for the call letter proper whenever it gets issued. That request was graciously granted, in view of what happened the previous year. In other words, these staffers saw first all the transaction letters concerning their FTC course before the Ministry's File Registry did. The schedule officer in the Administrative (Personnel) Section was carrying these documents to the Registry for proper filing, and taking them with him for action.

In the end, CD attended this elusive FTC; passed in flying colors; and was eventually upgraded a **Stenographer Grade II** since there were open vacancies for these positions. Achieving this all-important FTC graduation and the attendant change of status then triggered the need for more upward movements. Why not - and whoever rests on his oars? Stenographer Grade 2 was just the beginning position of that cadre and so one should naturally aspire to be promoted to grade 1 and up to Secretary Typist (as it was then called).

In the real sense, there ought not to be any problem about upward movements, because in the Civil Service, promotion normally comes in regular intervals of about two years after employment; but the secretarial cadre was operated under different rules and regulations. Just as it was with the Typists, under that cadre's special regulation, promotion must not be automatic, but must depend upon one passing higher examinations to merit upward movements. In the case of Stenographers, this implied going back to the FTC for these higher exams.

This was an apparent man's inhumanity to man, because the subjects were just the same. Only shorthand needed higher speeds of 100 wpm and 120 wpm respectively, but there was no new addition to Office Routine, Secretarial Practice, English Language, and Government Regulations. Moreover, typing remains 50 wpm as the highest requirement. Besides, in the office, no boss dictates at speeds up to 80 words per minute as they would not be reading from any script but only struggling to form sentence from the brain. How can one under that situation talk in speed? Where high speed in shorthand was needed at that time, was in the Parliament; and people in this group were specially trained to write at the speed of 140 words per minute to be called Verbatim Reporters.

In any case, for those in CD's situation, the meaning is that one must go back to the institution at intervals to read for and pass these same subjects at the same levels, with the exception of shorthand 100 wpm and typing 50 wpm for Stenographer Grade 1; and again go back whenever it became necessary to be upgraded when one would need to pass shorthand at the speed of 120 wpm, but still to be tested in typing at the same speed of 50 wpm to be upgraded as a Secretary-Typist, later renamed Confidential Secretary. This was CD's **Stumbling Block Number 8.** Yet he just kept on smiling.

> When we fall on the ground it hurts us,
> but we also need to rely on the ground
> to get back up.
> -Kathleen McDonald

BLOCK NUMBER 9

DISCRIMINATORY LAWS IN THE CIVIL SERVICE

Since this was already known, it did not arouse any shocks at all. It was not meant to stop one; but intended purely to slow down movement. As the pattern had always been to frustrate people, a new law came into effect, stipulating that after getting to stenographer Grade 2 level, one must remain there for two years before qualifying to undergo another course for the next grade (Stenographer Grade 1); and another two years must elapse before one should be allowed to go in for Secretary-Typists' course. Since the Federal Training Center was the only institution offering these courses, one had no alternative but to suffer under this CD's *Block Number 9*.

Meanwhile, soon after leaving the copy-typist cadre which in CD's time terminated on salary Grade Level 04, the Copy Typists Union put up a fight so sternly that approval was given for them to run a through scale, from Grade Level 01 to 03 without having to pass any further typing examination. In addition, after attaining Grade Level 3, one would be eligible for promotion into the position of Chief Typist on

Grade Level 04, from where that one's pay could continue to move up to salary grade level 08 (an executive position)!

The original schedule of progression formulated specially for this category of workers that the union fought successfully to abolish was as follows:

1. One had to get 25 words per minute (wpm) to be called a Typist Grade 3 on Grade Level F1;
2. Get 35 wpm for typist Grade 2 on Grade Level F2; and
3. Get 50 wpm for Typist Grade 1 on Grade Level F3.

Since promotion was dependent on one passing higher speed, one must remain stagnant on the beginning Grade level as long as one was unable to pass higher speeds; and the union not only successfully fought against this, but also got additional higher rank of Chief Typist on Salary Grade Level F4. Further fight later granted them upward movement to the executive Grade Level 08. The only implication in this is that one had to be in one grade for several years to reach the last pay level, before jumping to the next grade's pay level, and so on and so forth.

Were the stumbling blocks a blessing in disguise? Could they have held on a little longer? That is food for thought. But then my friend, CD would not like to subject himself to mark time for donkey's years to go on snail-speed through one scale that runs for about five years to another with relatively pea-nut annual salary increase. In any case, my friend wanted to move ahead, urged by the wise counsel of Denis Waitley:

> Determination gives you the resolve
> to keep going despite the road-
> blocks that lay before you.
> -*Denis Waitley*

At least he enjoyed gaining more knowledge even though there would be no material gain at the time to back it up; and who knows, laws may change tomorrow in his favor, as Daniel Webster said, when advised against being a lawyer: "There is always room at the top". Moreover, as indicated above, the time one would spend waiting to move on to Grade Level 08 was of course far too long for a progressive-minded person.

In addition to the absurdities of different laws favoring different categories of workers, in the same Civil Service, some personnel – mainly women - in the country's Foreign Service who knew next to nothing about typing and shorthand, were flown to European cities - France, Germany, Russia, and Portugal - to study as Bilingual Secretaries. Thus, in just two years, these fellows were returned and catapulted to salary Grade Level 07. It mattered not if what they came back with was only an amateurish knowledge of typing and shorthand, and the rudimentary knowledge of the language of the country where the course was undertaken. Very surprised at this state of affairs CD was really distressed, yet he still refused to envy their luck, and stayed smiling.

> If you fail to prepare,
> you're prepared to fail. - *Mark Spitz*

BLOCK NUMBER 10

MUSIC AS ALTERNATIVE?

Traditional Music

Somewhere along the line, CD found himself face to face with indecision; and whether to continue in the Civil Service, or branch out completely posed a jigsaw puzzle for him. When things were not moving as fast as he would want, the decision to remain in the civil service, or branch out completely to the music line crowded my friend's brain. In the first place, he was so involved in native water-pot-drumming, which in fact could be considered as his first profession. He had before the Lagos adventure, started playing this drumming for societies at home and in neighboring towns, because such drummers were scarce and had always remained in demand. In addition to the water-pot drumming, he also played nearly all the traditional music instruments for masquerades.

However, although in great demand, the stark reality of the low esteem held for the water-pot especially, and the other brands of traditional music in general, puts serious minded drummers off, as people in that profession, which services were only required mostly by dancing women, never progressed.

This is so because generally the demand occurs seasonally, like Christmas period. During this time, business booms as several dancing parties will be struggling to employ the services of the drummers who are in short supply; but after the season, drummers become jobless till the next festive season. Occasionally here and there, ceremonies do take place – like high society funeral, wedding, house warming or a visiting "god" dancing, etc. But earnings from such irregular occasions can hardly be relied upon to sustain one.

But since the show must go on in communities outside the Kalabari nation, CD performed his drumming arts that include Kuku (Clay-Pot) drums, Ekine-Sekiapu drums; Alili drums, Okolo-kuru-kuru drums, and Arungu masquerade drums for several Kalabari groups; as well as other Rivers communities and organizations in that city within a period spanning twenty-two years. Following are the groups CD played for:

1. **Kalabari Belema Ogbo, Lagos (a mixed gender society)**
   Clay Pot drumming for singing on the radio and cultural mermaid dancers
2. **Kalabari Community (Mermaid Dancers) Lagos -**
   Clay Pot drumming for: –
   - Mermaid dancers on Nigerian independence celebrations.
   - Mermaid dance on Reception in honor of Chief GKJ Amachree and Ambassador Joe Iyalla, on their appointments as UN Under-Secretary-General; and Nigeria's Ambassador to the United Nations, New York City, respectively.
3. **Kalabari Mermaid Dancers, Apapa (Ajegunle), Lagos:**
   Clay Pot drumming – for Cultural Mermaid Dance

4. **Kalaḅarị Arụngụ Society –**
   Arụngụ drumming for masquerade display
5. **Kalaḅarị Iḅianga Cultural Society Apapa (Ajegunle), Lagos**
   Clay Pot and Arụngụ drumming – for (Record waxing)
6. **Kalaḅarị Community, Ibadan**
   Clay Pot drumming – for Mermaid Dancers.
7. **Kalaḅarị Orumadọkụbọ Society, Lagos**
   Clay Pot drumming – for the aristocratic, romantic mixed society; and *Irịa* dances of the Kalabari people.
8. **Nyemọnị Improvement Society (NIS) (Mermaid Dancers) Lagos**
   Clay Pot drumming – for Cultural *Irịa* and Mermaid Dance shows to raise funds for general cultural shows and developmental projects.
9. **Buguma Improvement Association (BIAS) (Mermaid Dancers) Lagos**
   Clay Pot drumming – for Cultural *Irịa* and Mermaid Dance shows for fund raising for town improvement, etc.
10. **Buguma *Amaḅiḅi* Society (Mermaid Dancers) Lagos**
    Clay Pot drumming – for Buguma Youth organization cultural mermaid dance shows.
11. **Bakana Community, Lagos**
    Clay Pot and Masquerade drumming for Fund-raising show for St. Scholastica Secondary School establishment
    - Mermaid Dancers
    - *Imgbula* masquerade display
    - *Seki* masquerade display
12. **Pioneers Society of Bakana**
    Okolo-krukru masquerade display in honor of Mr. Tasie Braide for self-funding electricity supply to Bakana.

13. **Obama Women's Association, Lagos (OWAL)**

    Clay Pot drumming – for
    - Mermaid Dance shows to raise funds for town improvement;
    - Mermaid Dance for Steve Rhodes shows at the National Theatre

14. **Okrika Community, Lagos**
    - Clay Pot drumming – for Cultural Mermaid Dance shows.
    - Clay Pot drumming for Mermaid Dancers at the launching, in Port Harcourt, of "**Opu Jaja**" Opera – by Adam Fiberesima)

15. **Nembe Community, Lagos**

    Clay Pot drumming for Mermaid Dancers (Groups 1 & 2).

16. **Bonny (Okoloba) Community, Lagos -**

    Clay Pot drumming for Mermaid Dancers

17. **Rivers Community (Mermaid Dancers), Lagos –**

    Clay Pot drumming for:
    - Celebration of the Creation of Rivers State.
    - All Africa Festival of Arts in Algiers, Algeria (Won Bronze Medal)

18. **Queen's College Yaba, Lagos**

    Clay Pot drumming – for Rivers girls' students in cultural show

19. **Silver Birch, Psychic Sanctuary, Lagos (Mermaid Dancers)**

    Clay Pot drumming – for Music and Dance Festival – National Arts Theatre

High Life Music

Remarkably, apart from these traditional drumming, CD also had modern instrumental music talent which became his second profession, and was in fact, more profitable that could have made a huge difference for him, if he was in a well-organized society. The elementary school where the young man got his Primary School Certificate also had a Brass Band in which he was picked to be one of the "Band Boys". CD went to Lagos also with the knowledge acquired in that band, and sooner than expected, an old friend saw him and drafted him into the orchestra he was the trumpeter; and musically well talented, CD soon became a celebrated Trombonist.

This additional talent made the young man to work "24/7" as he went from the office in day time, to the hotel in the night to play music. With these two different types of music playing, my friend's part-time earnings almost doubled his Civil Service salary. The irony however, is that though the pay was good and the job enjoyable, they were not steady employments, as explained above, and had no future prospect, because jobs come and go without notice. So, how then could CD leave a stable but poorly paid Civil Service job for an unpredictable but lucrative music scene, became his dilemma.

At last, after careful consideration and evaluation of the seemingly insurmountable blocks lying in wait for him in the Civil Service, the young man eventually decided he would call it quits with the civil service. He, however, hung the final movement upon one condition; and that was only when he would have made a significant head way in the "Highlife Music" field.

Since the mind was already made up, the time CD thought was it came, and he was ready to wax some small "High-Life" music plates, which were expected to launch him into stardom. But just then **block number 10** struck. After promising him his first recording session, the

Artiste Manager of the recording company, died with his wife in a motor accident. His deputy, who automatically took over control of the studio and artistes' matters, agreed to sign CD on, but for some inexplicable reasons, slammed an obnoxious condition, which said that all the records that would come out at the first recording session, would be regarded as "audition case," which would not attract any royalty for CD!

But my friend was so overwhelmed with the prospect of having his music waxed that he failed to contemplate on the implications of the rather wicked condition, for which mistake he paid dearly. The records (two of them) came out at a very propitious time; as they were dedicated to a compatriot music legend-friend of his, who died early also in a motor accident; and his mother land, which was sacked by a secessionists group for non-cooperation during the country's civil war.

The records sold in thousands, and the company profited. Well-wishers urged CD on in person and through letters, not to waste any more time with the Civil Service, but to make music his full-time career. Little did they know how poorer my friend became by the very music discs they were hailing. For the disappointment he suffered at this recording company, CD moved his recording contract to the then only rival company in that country. But this second group of discs, sponsored only by a friend, could not hit the charts as the first two did. Moreover, a cousin of CD's, who was one of those urging him to make music a full-time carrier, and who had earlier voluntarily offered to buy my friend a set of musical instruments to start off, suddenly developed cold feet.

Realizing in a harsh way the full meaning of the saying that "a bird in hand is worth two in the bush," CD quickly abandoned his move to make music a full-time profession. Thus, my friend's intended plunge into music as profession hit the rocks as a result of this **block number 10.** But CD still kept his smiling face.

You cannot prevent the birds of sorrow from flying over your head;
but you can prevent them from building nests in your hair.
-Chinese Proverb

BLOCK NUMBER 11

APARTHEID IN THE COUNTRY'S FOREIGN SERVICE

Foreign Service Experience

Back fully to the Civil Service, CD knew that he was in want of greener pastures, and the answer, he reasoned, was in the country's Foreign Service that sends officers abroad on diplomatic duties, with secretarial staff presenting quick and constant posting necessities. He put in application for service transfer from the Radio Corporation where he was employed, but during the long wait for a positive response he consulted many compatriots who were already in that Ministry. Five of them were most prominent among them, with three Confidential Secretaries (Nimitẹin, Opu-da, and Mangi; *and* two Executive officers *(Ìlọmabọ and* Nyankpọ). As if by conspiracy, all of them gave CD varied versions of chilling disclosures about the sorry state of affairs in that branch of the country's government.

They all laughed, as if in unison, at CD's ignorance and pitied his decision of wanting to move to that Foreign Service; reminding him of the saying that "all that glitters is not gold." They, at different times and locations, further hinted him that several officers who were not in the core diplomatic cadre had left the Foreign Service in disgust and frustration for the bizarre service conditions operating there. When they saw that CD was interested to know more, they opened up; asking him if he knew that *apartheid* system was in practice at that Ministry?! He was startled; wondering why and how an arm of government deeply involved in the country's fight against that policy in Southern Africa then, could do the same thing.

They all went further to give graphic description of the goings-on in the Foreign Service; stating that in there, officers were divided into four categories called "Branches A, B, C, and D." Branch D was the technical, and Communications, and Diplomatic Courier staff; Secretarial staff alone belonged to Branch C; the Executive cadre qualified for Branch B; while the Administrative/Political Officer cadre belonged to the elitist Branch A. In other words, the people in Branch A were the only ones recognized as **diplomats**, while all others belonged to subordinate position, and branded Attachés in diplomatic missions abroad. This division of branches is enforced by the color of their passports. Diplomats carried **diplomatic** Passports with color Red; and all others must contend with the Official Passport with dark-blue color. It must be noted that this policy of discriminative passport is not backed by the United Nations Organization which is the custodian of international diplomacy, that gives all its employees abroad, one color passport - Green - irrespective of what they do. That was not all. Foreign Service allowances dished out to those at posts were designed to fluctuate according to the branches; so, in that accord Branch A's *Foreign Service, *Clothing, and *Children Allowances, were the highest; followed in descending order in Branches B, C, and D.

According to C.D.'s informants, the absurdity of this *apartheid* policy was felt in all its ramifications, and appeals made on several occasions to redress them fell on stone-deaf ears. Giving just a few illustrations, they stressed that all officers, irrespective of their branch get posted to Missions and suffer the same adverse conditions of the place – be it harsh weather, cost of living, cultural and racial hostility. Moreover, they wear the same type of dresses that carry identical prices. But the adverse effects were worse for those in the other branches as their blue passports hardly entitled them diplomatic recognition. It never mattered what work they did for the Mission. There were instances whereby host security services beat, harassed, and detained them, sometimes with diplomatic bags in their possession. Of course, it suited that country's proud diplomat to be given such opportunity to come to the rescue of his less fortunate colleague in the hands of his host security personnel, and the matter would die there. On the other hand, if any such attack happened to a "diplomat," the matter would reach the Foreign Office and also reported to Headquarters that would request for proper investigation and appropriate apology or retaliatory action if warranted.

Furthermore, in some countries that practiced socialist policies like the then Soviet Union, Cuba, China, and North Korea, only those who held diplomatic passports were allowed to shop in the single diplomatic retail store. This means all others with Official Passports must be prostrating to their diplomat-colleagues to help buy essential items for them, or else they and their family would have to make do with what they could see in the local markets at exorbitant prices. In many cases some essential items would not even be available locally.

This first-hand dreadful information from familiar people really jolted CD and posed as his **Stumbling Block Number 11**; yet he shrugged it off as ill-intentioned to prevent him from tasting what these confidants were enjoying in the Diplomatic Service. At least they were going out of the country and earning foreign currency. At that time, and till now, it has been a blessing to go overseas. It is an experience that entitles anyone in that position to earn, in the country's general parlance, the title of a "Been to."

So, CD reasoned if indeed he found any of these stories to be true, he would work hard in order not to stay long and suffer as Attaché. He would redouble efforts to read when lucky to be posted abroad, for at least a Bachelor's degree in any subject, and that would entitle him to be converted a "diplomat" too. After all, in those days, many of the "diplomats" from some parts of the country read only Arabic in the university! With that state of mind, my friend looked forward to seeing the situation personally. He reasoned that these "friends" were not the only people in the Foreign Service, and if others could withstand the so-called horrible conditions, why would CD not be able to do so. With this determination, CD remained smiling through **Block 11.**

If you want to see the sun shine,
you have to weather the storm.
- Frank Lane

BLOCK NUMBER 12

TRANSFER APPLICATION GOT MISSING IN THE FPSC

The compelling reason to go abroad and have the opportunity to further his education, was indeed the motivating factor that made CD finally apply for transfer of service to the Ministry of Foreign Affairs. At that time, the Secretarial cadre was pooled in the Ministry of Establishments, and officers were posted to different branches of government from time to time. But because the Foreign Ministry, being in charge of the diplomatic service, was semi-autonomous, movement to there was deemed to be inter-service transfers; and applications for such transfer of service had to go through the Federal Public Service Commission - FPSC (as it was called then). In compliance, CD forwarded his application to the FPSC; but the letter got abandoned at the file registry, and no one noticed!

After more than a year and nothing heard, CD came to the point of convincing himself that maybe what these guys told him were true, and that God would not want him undertake that transfer, hence the response was not forthcoming. But just as he was agreeing with that feeling not to make any move to trace the whereabouts of his transfer application, another colleague of his at the Broadcasting House, who also applied and pursued his letter to the Public Service Commission, discovered where CD's was left abandoned. On his return to the office the man approached my friend with the good news that his application was still alive in the forgotten heap of documents at the Federal Public Commission. Describing where exactly he saw this letter, the man urged CD to go for it, and not be discouraged.

My friend took this as God's immediate answer to his wrong interpretation, and called at the FPSC office, and after several searches, his letter was dug out just as his comrade told him, under a pile of other abandoned papers. Being who he is, CD controlled his anger, and appealed to the officer in charge to please forward the application to its destination without further delay. The officer indeed felt humiliated, but was forced to take action. Bravo; within a short period of time, my friend got a call from the Foreign Office to come for interview!

The interview at the Foreign Ministry went well; my friend was accepted, and the transfer process was so smooth that within a short space of time, CD reported for duty at the administration Department of the country's Ministry of Foreign Affairs. Obviously **Block Number 12** was put in place for him to wait for God's time to move over; and so, CD kept going in smiles.

> The elevator to success is out of order.
> You'll have to use the stairs -
> one step at a time
> -Joe Girard

BLOCK NUMBER 13

BEAST OF BURDEN

On settling down at the Foreign Ministry, my friend soon confirmed that the stories as told by his friends were in fact understatements! In short, these guys perhaps had no time to mention two very problematic goings-on which include the "beast of burden" nature of the Secretarial cadre in that arm of government, as well as the slow nature of upward movement as it affected them.

The first thing CD discovered on arrival in the Ministry was the fact that the Confidential Secretary who earned the fanciful title of Archivist or Administrative Attaché at Post, was a real beast of burden, who in a typical Mission when posted abroad, was scheduled to tackle the following duties and functions:

Secretarial Duties:

1. Keeping the File Registry (Open and Classified);
2. Communications;
3. Diplomatic Bag;
4. Administrative duties;

5. Consular Matters;
6. Protocol duties;
7. Security duties.

If one thinks the list of an officer's duties is long and frightening, that one should wait until he or she sees details involved in the full description given below of what this beast of burden does in a typical diplomatic mission.

1. **Secretarial Duties**

    Since there are locally recruited secretarial staffers, what were compulsory for this "home-based" officer to handle were classified, which included:
    a) The Ambassador's Dispatches
    b) Political, Economic, Annual and Post Reports.
    c) *Notes-Verbale* (official diplomatic correspondence), and
    d) All day-to-day confidential and secret telegrams, letters, minutes and Aide-Memoirs.

    It is obvious that these typing materials are in volumes. Yet they must be typed by the single "home-based" Secretary from the draft stage to its final production, which included stencil cutting. At CD's time, there was no memory typewriter, nor computer to work with; so, every single piece must be typed afresh. Thus, before one report went out, it had been typed seven times or more, depending on how sound the writers were. This state of affairs notwithstanding, the almighty "diplomats'" inability to distinguish between what should be classified and what should be an open document, would still insist that all documents, from its draft forms to final copy, must be typed by this unfortunate Secretary.

2. **File Registry (Open and Classified)**

The Secretary keeps the File Registry. He/she is not only expected to keep the files up-to-date, but also required to file all papers correctly and bring forth promptly any matter called for. No Messenger was allowed to touch classified files or documents, so he/she had to personally carry files to and from offices. He/she must be an impudent rascal who dared to ask a "diplomat," who could be four grade levels below him/her, to come to the Registry for a file. All a "diplomat" need do was just call on the telephone for file so-and-so, and it must be taken there on time.

3. **Communications**

For economic reasons, Communications Officers were not posted to 90% of the country's diplomatic missions abroad. So, in spite of all his/her burdens, the Secretary is still found to be best suited to handle communications duties. He/she must have been rushed through a crash 4-week training only to encode and decode classified messages. No technical know-how of the machine he/she was to work with was imparted to him/her. This officer's other very pressing assignments notwithstanding, he/she was expected to send and process received messages promptly. To encode and decode classified messages required several hours of painstaking and strictly concentrative work. In the developed world, machines such as Electro-Cipher System (ECS) were used to encipher and decipher documents within minutes, thereby making it easier for the over-burden staff. But the well-known psyche of that country to see a fellow undergo great difficulties at all times, no effort was made to let these machines go round all the Missions. And so, the beast of burden was sometimes left to virtually sleep in the office, trying to encode or decode a long message to and from Headquarters!

All this means that the Secretary hardly could afford the luxury of a day's absence from work. No, he/she would throw the mission's functions into a grinding halt. Conversely, even a Head of Mission (Ambassador) could afford to go on vacation without any adverse effect on the functions of the Mission. Missions at certain times, remained, and functioned properly several years without a substantive ambassador.

4. **Diplomatic Bag**

Due also to economic constraints, Diplomatic Couriers were posted to very few Missions abroad, and so diplomatic bag duties were imposed upon the Secretary. This covered scheduling mails, tying bags and taking them to the airport for conveyance to Headquarters. This officer also calls at the airport to collect in-coming bags from either a transiting Courier, or a Pilot of the approved carrying airliner. The importance of the cargo he/she carried enforced that he/she must enter into the arrival point of the airport to reach the Pilot. But this unfortunate Secretary is unlucky to be posted to a country where the blue "Official" Passport he/she was holding, was not given diplomatic recognition, so he/she had to go through the ritualistic ordeal twice a week trying to plead, beg, or smuggle himself/herself in and out of the lounge. This is the time when if he/she is unfortunate to meet uncompromising security officials, he/she would be denied entry; or if he/she insisted, would be punched and kicked out. There had been times when an officer had been put behind bars and the sacred pouch in his/her possession seized, only to be released the following day after a "diplomat" from the mission had intervened.

Ironically, Couriers, who were below the Secretary in qualification and the weight of duties they perform, were given Diplomatic Passport, just to carry this cargo. But due to lack of fund, these officers were posted only to a very few selected Missions, e.g., London, Washington, New York, and Moscow. Thus, the bulk of missions, about 99.9% all over the world, that had no Courier service, were covered by the over-burdened Secretaries, and yet these workers were not accorded diplomatic status!

5. **Administration**

The Secretary was called Administrative *Attaché*, so, in addition to being Personal Assistant to the Ambassador, he/she doubled as the Assistant to the Head of Chancery in diverse areas. In this typical mission under focus, he/she virtually performed all the daily running of the mission, because the incumbent Head of Chancery, who knew little or nothing, depended on the ubiquitous Secretary. The Secretary would write letters; supervise local staff, as well as Drivers and the vehicles they drive. He/she would keep the stationery store; serve as the mail-runner – shuttling to and from post offices; and maintain the post office franking machine.

6. **Consular Matters**

　　At CD's time, immigration services were handled by the Foreign Ministry, which was handling the issuance of passports at Headquarters. That makes diplomatic missions abroad to be handling to all such Immigration duties; and the ubiquitous Secretary had to cover it all; which include:

　　a) issuing visas to foreigners intending to visit his/her country;
　　b) issuing and renewing passports to fellow country citizens; and
　　c) keeping his/her compatriots out of trouble in that foreign land.

　　The not-too-favorable reputation of his/her countrymen and women abroad ensured that this officer always had a hard task dealing with the host country's Police and Immigration officials.

　　Later, due to pressures from the Internal Affairs Ministry, these consular duties were taken over, and immigration personnel from that Ministry began getting posted to some key missions abroad to handle these duties. Yet, many missions that did not have the privilege of having the required Immigration Officers, the all-weather Secretary remained the one to continue acting as the Consular Officer.

7. **Protocol**

　　It is the lot of the Secretary in this Mission on trial, to see in and out visiting officials and ranking nationals of his/her dear country. The difficulty in getting messages in and out of the country, as well as flight delays and booking irregularities, pose very formidable factors that ensure that this officer sleeps at the airport in most times waiting for a never arriving official.

8. **Security Officer**

Due also to economic constraints, Chancery Guards are not sent to 99.9 per cent of missions abroad. The chancery Guard's work naturally falls on the jack-of-all-trades Secretary. It is his/her responsibility to come first – latest 30 minutes earlier than the official opening hour – to open the doors of the chancery to let local staff in. He/she has no closing hours. On very rare days, he/she might be lucky to close one hour after the official closing time, to see that everybody was gone, to lock the doors.

Normally, of course, in a small mission that has only one "home-based Secretary, he/she has to wait for the boss (Ambassador). Woe betides him/her on days that the Ambassador had to assume work two hours before closing time, because he had been "consulting colleagues" (this happens almost daily throughout CD's tenure in this particular mission!); or to wait in the office for the Ambassador's official dinner scheduled for 8 o'clock in the evening. This was because as His/Her Excellency's residence is several miles away in the suburbs, the Ambassador would not be able to go home and come back to the city for such dinner appointment. In contrast, the Secretary's "diplomat" counterparts, and other Attachés, come and leave the office at their own time.

This may sound incredible, but it is unfortunately true. In the whole world where that country established diplomatic missions, only London, New York, Washington, and Paris, had nearly fully staff; while all others were short-staffed, and officers forced to undertake more than one schedule. That means when the few diplomatic officers in those short-staffed missions are confined to undertake purely diplomatic duties, the rest must fall on Branch B officers, and there lied the problem.

Due to liquidity crunch, Executive Officers, Couriers, and Communication officers would be left at home, yearning for posting; while all the above enumerated duties are heaped upon the unfortunate Confidential Secretary. Even then, CD had no choice but to smile through these daunting tasks under this ***Block Number 13*** when he came face to face with them.

<blockquote>
Do not pray for easy lives.
Pray to be stronger men.
Do not pray for tasks equal to your powers.
Pray for powers equal to your tasks.
- Phillips Brooks
</blockquote>

BLOCK NUMBER 14

DEARTH OF VACANCIES

With luck, CD's fortitude began to pay off gradually. Just at the beginning of his early days at the Foreign Service, a new civilian administration came into being; and a good number of well-meaning personalities within the Ministry were able to attract the ears of the new boss to look into the anomalies going on at the Ministry he had just been sworn in to lead. With God on their side, this boss immediately yielded to the outcry and curtailed the four branches (A, B, C & D) into just two (A and B). In the new dispensation, this means the elitist officers retained their branch A, while all others were joined together in Branch B). There were also far-reaching innovations in favor of the B branch. Although still left in that segregated branch, the new rule favored them to earn Foreign Service, as well as clothing allowance, according to their official salary grade levels instead of their branch as was the case before.

This feat was achieved because the hitherto super-power Directors-General (Permanent Secretaries) of government Ministries lost their supremacy handed to them by the colonialists when they transferred power at independence. That power was held tenaciously until a military government took power and put military Ministers as head. So, after a long military rule ended and civilians eventually returned to power, the headship of Ministries had become so entrenched in favor of Ministers that the Permanent Secretaries (now Directors-General) could no longer regain what they thought to be their heritage.

However, having scaled all the required trainings and qualifications, and attained the rank of Confidential Secretary on Salary Grade Level 07 by the time he transferred to the foreign Service, one would only be promoted to higher grades after every two years as it was done in other arms of government. But being a service of its own, lack of vacancies kept CD waiting on one grade level for seven years! Ironically, while his branch of secretaries had to wait that long for one promotion to grade level 08, his lucky other colleagues titled "Bilingual Secretaries", had enough vacancies to move into, and in short space of years, up to grade level 12, far and above Confidential Secretaries! But even this ***stumbling block number 14*** did not succeed in affecting any change in CD's smiling countenance.

> You never will be the person you can be
> if pressure, tension, and discipline
> are taken out of your life.
> -James, G. Bilkey

BLOCK NUMBER 15

NO OVERSEAS POSTING FOR CD

As noted earlier, on transfer to the Foreign Office, CD was first employed at one of the Administrative Offices, but just within a month, he was called to replace someone at the Minister's Office, who was going abroad on official posting. Quite new to the foreign office set up, it was daunting for my friend to adapt so quickly and perform his duties as expected. No one knew that it was my friend's very first stint in a foreign office setting, as all around him thought he too was part of them just returning from overseas posting. Indeed, to be thrown into such a sensitive office without adequate orientation was quite demanding for CD; but he was quite up to the task; having been trained about what to expect as a Secretary in all office environments. He did so good that even old hands who were higher in rank than he was were placed under him, as the Minister preferred dealing with CD to anyone else.

Completely settled down at the Foreign Office, and still smiling at the situation going on there, CD wondered when would be the time to get rid of the secretarial profession and its nasty experience. However, he encouraged himself to persevere a little longer, and not forget what he had aimed for; which was to use the Foreign Service as a spring board to further his education. It was reassuring that government encouraged its employees to improve their knowledge, and CD had earlier got his GCE (GED) in anticipation, because the probability of going abroad was then very real. It had thus gone beyond the point of rethinking about being there and jeopardizing his chances of improving his education. More encouraging was when CD saw in the Department, and also heard about several officers who had utilized the opportunity of their foreign posting to improve their education and got converted to the elitist diplomatic cadre. But as usual, CD did not know that **block number 15** was laying ambush for him.

My friend became due for posting; and the Posting Committee met several times, finding his name among those due for going abroad. The time was very apt too, as his boss, a military Foreign Minister was, himself retiring from service in readiness for the in-coming civilian administration. Between the time of announcing the postings and the time the Minister would leave government for good, was only a difference of one month. But alas, without any attempt to seek the opinion of the boss, the posting committee dropped CD's name from the list with the argument that "If he was posted away at the time, the boss would be displeased!" The boss eventually left, but my friend had to wait, still smiling for another whole year because **Block Number 15** refused to go away.

> There never was night that had no morn.
> -*Dinah Maria Mulock Craik*

BLOCK NUMBER 16

TERTIARY EDUCATION IMPEDED

My friend's determination to improve himself against all odds forced him to read for his General Certificate of Education (GCE) or GED. That was a young man, working twenty-four hours a day; yet he could make time to study for this certificate and got it! He was inspired by this statement:

> I will read and improve myself;
> for one day, I know my time will come.
> -*Abraham Lincoln*

So, when his time came the following year, CD got Foreign Service Posting Orders, without any hindrance. So, when the year's posting exercise came up, the new God-sent civilian Foreign Minister boss - a man of policy who could not be easily swayed except he was personally convinced - made it impossible for the usual "Minister's consent might not be given" concept to stand. The Honorable Minister disagreed with that advice, and allowed CD to go! Thus, that time around, my friend was not only posted, but also had his choice of place - New York City, where the opportunity to get admission to institutions of higher education were easier. He chose that city because the Minister had during the year taken him there for the United Nations General Assembly meeting. It was a very auspicious trip which also saw his country's President, addressing the United Nations General Assembly (UNGA), and the trip afforded CD the opportunity to explore schools to attend if and when he ever arrived there on posting.

The very first week he arrived New York City, and still in the hotel, pending the time the accommodation for him would be ready, CD went straight to register at a reputable College, which offered evening classes. Courses would start at 6 o'clock in the evening after office hours, and end at 9 o'clock, and my friend fought very hard to leave the office in time to meet up on daily bases.

Indeed, the obstacles were daunting, as one was expected on daily basis when the United Nations General Assembly (UNGA) would be in session, to stay back in the office to write reports to Headquarters. Even when it was not time for UNGA, his boss - the Permanent Representative - would go to late meetings or Dinner with fellow Ambassadors, and so would expect CD to wait behind till he returned to sign pending reports for transmission to Headquarters. Since that was what took him to New York, and not education, my friend had to suffer the discouraging antics of the Ambassador, until sooner than expected that impeding Ambassador was posted back to headquarters.

Finally, after ignoring all the allurements of the Big Apple's niceties, and reading through summer to fall; and also ignoring the pain of the exorbitant school fees and textbooks, as well as the heavy duty at the office, CD made his papers in record three years; making the National Dean's List twice, and graduated with a Bachelor's degree in Political Science! He confided in me that throughout the process, one of his sources of encouragement was a Hindu principle that says:

> "There is no greater dignity than that of the man who declares, 'I will never cease in laboring to advance my family.' Perseverance and sound understanding - these two are what exalt a man's family. When a man declares he will advance his family, God Himself will wrap His robes and lead the way."

Recognition must be accorded here to his life-time friend - Martin Anyanwu - who helped him in more ways than one, to gain the college admission. Thus, for one born in such poor circumstances, these miraculous intercessions by the Almighty encouraged my friend to pursue his determination and perseverance to achieve his educational goal.

> Out of difficulties grow miracles.
> *-Jean de la BruyFe*

BLOCK NUMBER 17

CERTIFICATE EVALUATION STALLED!

Having acquired the Golden Fleece, he was elated and eager to return home to be converted in no time, to a career diplomat status; and be free from all the humiliations in Branch B.

Blinded by this enthusiasm, CD hit **block number 17** with a big bang! On his return to headquarters, and to his greatest shock, the foreign certificate evaluation department of the Federal Ministry of Education was not as enthusiastic to evaluate his certificate. This had nothing to do with the authenticity of his qualification. The school was a recognized one and CD attended as in-campus student – a new requirement then by the Government. His lady colleague, who was junior in rank to him, and who incidentally also had her education at the same school CD attended, had her certificate evaluated almost on the spot, and even without anyone bothering to call for her official transcripts.

But in CD's case, the very same evaluating officer kept asking for all sorts of documents and clarifications. My friend's requests to the school he attended in New York City forced the school to write stinkers to this lady, but instead of working on the papers, she got offended and decided to "sit" on it indefinitely.

My friend was later hinted that she might be expecting some "palm-greasing" before acting on the case. That information got CD so upset that he reported the matter to a higher officer in that Ministry, who as luck would have it, came from the same home-town with him. The boss attacked the lady desk-officer in the morning, and by that very afternoon, the letter of evaluation had been hand-carried to the desk of the schedule officer in my friend's Ministry. So, CD finally scaled this block, but then still **smiling on,** he failed to realize that **block** *number 18* was being skillfully rolled into place against him.

If you see ten troubles coming down the road,
you can be sure that nine will run into the ditch before they reach you.
-Calvin Coolidge

BLOCK NUMBER 18

NO MORE AGE EXEMPTIONS FOR NYSC

National Youth Service Corps (NYSC) is a one-year service put in place for university graduates to be posted to states other than theirs, with a view to familiarizing them with other parts of the country, in search of national unity. During its formulation it was misunderstood, and students, with secret instigation by some lecturers, suspecting government's ill-intentions, went on riot; protesting the idea of forcing them to undergo such a demeaning service after graduating from university. But now its effect has indeed made a lot of impact on the youths from all parts of the country that hitherto had had unfavorable views of other tribesmen and women.

Incidentally, CD was part of the delegation (as one of the Federal Education Minister's aides) to the first ever national meeting of eminent educationists at one of the country's reputable Universities. On arrival, the team found the atmosphere agitated. Posters of students with threatening slogans against the scheme were all over the campus. Young ones like CD mingled with some students, and were spared of their wrath when they eventually embarked on their riotous action. The meeting could not hold the following day, as students disrupted it by overturning tables and tearing into pieces all the papers meant for presentation.

The meeting was rescheduled, and later held at a different location, and NYSC came into being.

My friend never knew that the very institution he was part of in its set up stages would later deprive him of his heart's desire. At its inception, graduates who were already over thirty years old were exempted from the scheme; and at the time CD graduated in 1983, he was already above thirty, but yet he was not spared because the law was interpreted to affect only those who graduated from 1985, and not earlier. So, when the time for conversion/promotion interview was due, CD received his letter of invitation like all those affected. But as the date approached, he received another letter, rescheduling his interview for the following year after he must have completed his NYSC exercise. Apparently, the interview board got information about his scheduled NYSC service. This **Block Number 18** thus made sure that CD's conversion was delayed. Yet my friend shrugged it off with a smile.

> When it is dark enough,
> you can see the stars.
> -Charles A. Beard

BLOCK NUMBER 19

NYSC DEPRIVED CD OF CONVERSION

On the appointed day, CD reported at the Orientation Camp of the National Youth Service Corps he was assigned to, and completed the orientation in two weeks. After the orientation he returned to serve the one-year active service in his place of work, which was permitted for those who were already employed. At the end of the successful service my friend heaved a big sigh of relief after receiving his Discharge Certificate; rejoicing that finally, it was his turn to leave that "God-forsaken" secretarial profession for good. But bang! CD crashed into *Block Number 19.* No, this was more like a brick wall than ordinary block.

The pompous civilian Minister of Foreign Affairs at the helm of affairs issued a circular, shattering the hopes of all conversion-due staff, announcing that there would be no more conversion to the career diplomat cadre unless one was already on grade level twelve, and no more below. At the time, reaching grade level twelve by an officer in CD's cadre in the Foreign Office was like scoring a military victory over a super-power.

This is because the vacancy position on the said grade level was only twelve (12), and because that was his seventh year on Grade Level Nine (09), CD had no answer as to whether that was the end of the road as he would need to have two more promotions to get to level twelve. The levels were set up in a way that there was no Grade Level Eleven, as officers jump from grade level 10 to 12 on their next promotion. Once again, just because he must serve his National Youth Service Corps duties, a huge **Block Number 19** got enough time to role itself in between him and conversation to the Diplomatic Officers' cadre. But CD still managed to remain in his smiling mood.

> We can complain that rose bushes have thorns;
> or we can rejoice that thorn bushes have roses.
> *- Abraham Lincoln*

BLOCK NUMBER 20

CONVERSION GRADE LEVEL REVERSED DOWN!

After just a few years, the stagnation on one position was lifted, as steps were taken to increase vacancy positions in the Secretarial cadre. Also, as luck would have it, during that expansion exercise, the vacancy positions of grade level 12 were increased from 12 to 14. Perhaps, as was not unusual in that country, some powers-that-be did something to benefit vested interests. In any case, as a result of that increase, CD got promoted in quick succession to the sacred grade level 12, and now ready for the elusive conversion.

But then, it was too late for CD, because things had changed once again! Why not? Only God's laws are immutable; while man's laws are subject to change according to his whims and caprices. This time around, the law changed towards the opposite direction that earlier deprived my friend of conversion, because he was below the required grade level to be converted. Now, the story was that there had become too many grade-level 12 officers in the diplomatic officer cadre; and so only lower grade officers were, in reverse, needed for conversion!

This was a great blow, but there was nothing anyone could do about it. Under this circumstance, just as it was with the evaluation of certificate, CD's junior colleagues on grade level Nine (09) and eight (8) got converted, because he was that time around, too high for conversation. Yet still my friend managed to remain smiling!

> My imperfections and failures are as much
> a blessing from God as my successes and my talent;
> and I lay them both at His feet.
> -*Mohandas Gandhi*

BLOCK NUMBER 21

CONVERSION TIED TO ACADEMY ATTENDANCE

At this point it became quite apparent that someone somewhere was really scheming certain people out of Branch A – the elusive and elitist club. To ensure this was so, but to deceive the unsuspecting person that they meant well, additional block was rolled into place in reinforcement. Just as the Level Twelve vacancy situation got improved and the prospect of CD's conversion became quite apparent, a new rule was yet again issued, directing never to convert any serving officer unless and until he or she had undergone the Foreign Service Academy.

This new directive was unheard of before as this academy was set up since when the country achieved its independence, to conduct training for new graduate recruits. The policy was to appoint, or convert before academy, and not after. That means in clear language that new entrants and converts were first to be in office for some years, before attending the academy training, designed to acquaint employees of diplomatic ethics and practice.

The implications of this new rule tend to confirm the notion that the "Powers-That-Be" were bent on scheming some serving officers out of this "elitist" branch. Obviously, as a result of the fact that this category of staff had increased, a situation seen to be depriving candidates who pass through political god-fatherism, all sorts of measures had to be placed in effect to discourage more entrants. To achieve their desired harsh results, the authorities added the following more stringent attachments to the Foreign Service Academy Law:

1. The academy conducts its training program only once a year.
2. For serving officers under this rule, admission was not automatic; but by special recommendations.
3. Most importantly, even attendance of the academy would no longer guarantee immediate conversion. Availability of vacancy, and how well one performed in the course, takes over as criteria for determining one's chances of being converted.

That seemed to prove to be the end of the road for CD. But were all hopes for him to become a Branch-A Officer lost? The answer, to his surprise was "No". From out of the blues an appreciative female Ambassador, who he had served meritoriously, and who had been sympathetic to his plight, came home from her post for consultation, and used her influence to secure a place for him in the Academy that was about to begin. CD was not aware of this intervention, as the Ambassador decided to first convince the Director of the course before letting him know. When she was sure of securing the slot, she then went to break the good news to CD, and pleaded with him to disregard all the appeals for posting, and make sure he attended the course, to put paid to all their stalling tactics regarding his conversion. God bless this saintly woman. CD was very grateful for her thoughtfulness and promised to give the course a try.

However, before the course started, word went round that a posting exercise was already in motion and that CD's name had been picked as one of the affected officers. This development coming at that particular time, sent signal to CD that indeed the Great One above had better plans for him. So, after weighing the advantages and disadvantages of undergoing this course at the time of his career, my friend opted out and went on to what was destined to be his last posting in the country's Foreign Service. CD's one regret had been the fact that he could not see this lady ambassador ever since, to explain his reason for declining the offer after all her selfless efforts. CD hoped that she did not know of his refusal to attend; but if she by any chance got informed by the Director, prayed that she forgives him for showing such ungratefulness.

Indeed, that was the end of CD's desire to become a "diplomat" of that country. In fact, owing to the economic crunch the country was facing at that point in time, diplomats were wishing they were Attachés, especially those in the Secretarial and Finance cadres in Branch B. In addition to the economic problem, the tumultuous political situation in the country under a new military and more totalitarian regime contributed to the decision to drastically cut posting activities for the teaming diplomats. Some officers were staying back at headquarters for upward of seven years, with its attendant hardship. These officers, irrespective of their ranks, were begging and bribing for postings, while the Secretarial and Finance cadres were enjoying postings at will. So, CD remained in the service as a Branch B officer, enjoying postings as and when due and rising to Grade Level 13 before deciding to voluntarily retire at the end of in his last posting.

These overwhelming and astounding experiences in the Foreign Ministry that CD stumbled through in **Blocks 14** to **21** are indeed worthy of summarizing for in-depth understanding and appreciation.

1. Firstly, National Youth Service Corps (NYSC) deprived CD of his chance to be converted into the diplomatic cadre. At its inception, graduates over thirty years old were exempted from the scheme. CD was already above thirty when graduated, but

because he graduated in 1983 and the law affected only those who graduated from 1985, and not earlier, he was not spared. So, when the time for conversion/promotion interview came up, he was rescheduled for the following year after he must have completed his NYSC exercise.
2. Secondly, after CD got discharged from the NYSC exercise, conversion seemed to be overtaken by events! It used to be automatic for graduates of any subject as soon as one got a university degree to be converted. But when it came to CD's turn the law changed saying that there should be no more conversion to the career diplomat cadre unless one was already on grade level twelve (12), because all the grades lower than twelve had been over-staffed.
3. Thirdly, again the law reversed after CD attained Grade Level Twelve, because by then there had become too many officers in that grade level; and so only lower grade officers were needed! Under that obnoxious law, CD's junior colleagues on grade level nine (09) and below got converted, because he was, at that time around, too high for conversation!
4. Fourthly, just as the Level Twelve vacancy situation got improved, a new rule came into effect, not to convert any serving officer unless and until he or she had undergone the Foreign Service Academy! The practice since the creation of the Foreign Office was to appoint or convert before academy; and that was why new entrants went to the academy after they got already recruited.

Moreover, at that particular time, even attendance of the academy no longer guaranteed immediate conversion for one, as availability of vacancy and how well one performed in the course determined the officer's chances of being converted.

But overall, this outcome proves that denial of his quest for conversion from Branch B to Branch A, was indeed a blessing in disguise; because at that particular time, those in Branch A were no longer enjoying overseas posting due to current financial hardship faced by the country as a result of a dictatorial government in office and the resultant world sanctions. That made Branch A officers at Headquarters having kwashiorkor as a result of insufficiency of funds to take care of themselves and families. So, for CD, for not being converted to the diplomatic cadre in the country's Foreign Service, turned out to be in his advantage; and his smiles in this respect, turned into the last laugh!

> What I aspired to be;
> and was not,
> comforts me.
> *-Robert Browning*

BLOCK NUMBER 22

PENSIONS STUMBLING BLOCKS

Coming into the world after retirement, CD still had to contend with several blocks rolling into his path starting with the fight to get his retirement benefits and pension. Having been used to stumbling blocks, this really did not pose any surprise to my friend, as he already knew what he was up against. Nevertheless, for a retired person, he normally should expect his reduced pay to stay alive with his family.

But that was not the case for my friend. This young man worked for the government of his country for over twenty-five years, and qualified for monthly pension payments until he dies. But since things do not work so smoothly in that country, his pension matter was forgotten in the locker room. CD struggled for nine years before he could unlock the room at the Foreign Ministry to begin the process of preparing his pension papers, which would be forwarded to the Pension Office for final processing and payment.

However, CD was dead wrong thinking that the process would be smooth; because he was asked to produce papers about his progress while in service, to facilitate the processing of his retirement benefits. No well-organized country will ask an ex-employee to produce his/her particulars before payment of his/her retirement benefits. But in that country CD was asked to produce: the following:

1. Papers showing his first employment date!
2. Papers showing the date he transferred services to the Foreign Service;
3. Papers showing that he was not indebted to the government;
4. Papers showing dates of his last promotion; and
5. Papers showing gazette confirmation of his appointments!

Absurd as it sounded, CD had no alternative but to comply. Requests numbers 1 to 4 were submitted with great difficulties. But the hurdle that lasted for another four years, since CD was not stationed in the country, was the publication of his appointment confirmation in the official gazette. Helpless, my friend was led to a middle-man in the Office of the Head of Service, who was liaising with another man in the Office of the Government Printer. This was the only option since this fifth request could not be produced. Huge sums of money exchanged hands, and CD thought all was right for the publication to appear in less than three months, as the man assured. The result was disappointment as no publication containing the name - CD - ever appeared in the Gazette. The man gave several frivolous excuses till he ran out of any, and just disappeared into thin air.

My friend had to look for alternative help, and luckily, he found one right there in the Foreign Ministry who had helped several retirees to get their entitlements. This gentleman succeeded in working the papers through within the Ministry without any Gazette publication, and onward to the Office of the Head of Service where the gratuity and pension would be processed and paid.

However, another two years passed without any further movement because his file got missing in the Pension Office; and could only be found when CD's cousin found it under a pile of other forgotten files. The file was then put in the hands of a lady in that office, who helped to move it through a rigorous path, and CD was asked to come home from abroad to "personally sign" the voucher!

My friend travelled home, and discovered that even at that level, one still had to fight tooth and nail to ensure that one's file go through more than a dozen tables, and then to the Audit section manned by equal number of auditors struggling to share less than ten desks. Do not forget, something, of course, must be dropped on all these desks for one's file to move on! This is just the beginning, as the file must still go through a couple of higher tables before finally settling down on the almighty Director's desk. This insensitive Director enjoyed the sight of crowd of helpless pensioners sprawling around the corridors in front of his office, while he surrounded himself with praise-singers from both his department and his village, celebrating his birthday amidst clinking of champaign bottles and glasses with photographers snapping cameras at the celebrant and whoever was interested in a government office!

For this lack of empathy for elderly, sickly and impoverished pensioners, it normally would take at least two weeks before the "god" in the pension office would put his all-important signature on one's payment voucher after it eventually completed its rigmarole journey onto his desk. Finally, after a whole week passed, this Director signed CD's voucher which eventually was sent to one of the many Pensions Office Banks for payment.

But not so fast, CD! The Bank that was supposed to transfer the money into his own bank account began its own dragging of feet. First, an official told my friend to inform the pension office that its account with that bank was in the red! Surprised, CD still had to deliver the message, and after three days the elusive Director, ordered a subordinate to transfer certain amount to the Bank from "any of their banks" with sufficient money for payment of CD's batch of pensioners whose matters had been finally dealt with. In other words, CD was God-sent for those other less fortunate local pensioners whose vouchers got lucky to come into his batch.

Unbelievably, after this transfer was made, the Bank staffers diverted CD's money into their own deposit accounts and started to shift reasons for not paying the money into CD's account! First, they said the money was sent but returned without reason; and second, they said the reason was that the name on the bank account was not as exactly as displayed in the voucher! When CD enlisted his contact at his bank to investigate the cause of this money being returned, the lady expressed surprise at the reasons adduced by that Bank, and advised CD to ask from the Bank's staffer handling the matter with some specific questions.

With this advice, my friend confronted the bank's front-man to give more details of how and when the money was transferred and returned for his bank to launch an investigation. The man agreed but after promising to give the information on another day if only CD could call back, the point-man refused to pick calls. But lo; in less than a week after that, the next telephone call was from CD's bank, reporting that the account had been credited after three months.

So, in the end, after a lengthy period of nearly ten years of his retirement from the country's Civil Service, and the never-ending rigmarole within its Pension Office; and then in the private Bank, CD received his retirement gratuity and pension, and remained smiling this time, at the successful conclusion of a long and meandering **Block Number** *22*.

SMILING THROUGH STUMBLING BLOCKS

Losers see thunderstorms,
Winners see rainbows;
Losers see icy streets,
Winners put on their ice skates!
-- Denis Waitley

BLOCK NUMBER 23

NO MORE JOB OPPORTUNITIES FOR CD

Since it is man's portion to go through endless blocks in life, my friend, CD faced some more stumbling blocks after his exit from his country's Foreign Service, as discussed hereunder.

On arrival in the United States, and after a brief stay in New York City, CD travelled down to a small city in Texas bordering Mexico, where all attempts to secure a job became futile, and CD was advised to embark on further training, especially in the medical field. My friend took this advice seriously and enrolled in a technical institute to study Medical Assisting. The motivating factor in this trade choice was that the city had great need for personnel in this field, which attracted many compatriots from their former stations for what obviously was a greener pasture. While a few doctors, pharmacists and nurses got employed in hospitals and other medical facilities, a large number of them opened up their own private clinics and pharmacy outlets, and were doing very well. CD reasoned that after qualifying in about a year, there would be no problem in securing a job in one of these clinics owned by his fellow compatriots if any of the established hospitals were unable to employ him.

The training cost CD over thirteen thousand dollars ($13,000), borrowed from the school and government educational loan providers. The course went well; my friend graduated, and got official board certification on passing the prescribed tests. But bang! As usual, CD once again struck his two feet straight on this **Block Number 23**, as no institution would want to have him in their establishment. Even the clinics of his compatriots, which he placed very high hopes on, could do nothing for the man. Many reasons were adduced to refuse him employment, prominent among which was that he was a man, and only female Medical Assistants were required. The other reason was because the city being a predominantly Spanish-speaking one, only those who were bilingual qualified to be employed in their clinics, because most of the patients they attended to did not speak English, the only language CD speaks.

The irony of this permanent road-block in the Medical Assistant profession is that even though CD failed to secure any job for the position, he still had to be paying, seemingly for life, the huge loan taken for the training from the meager salary his wife was bringing home. After finishing the school side of it which was about three thousand dollars, the greater government part of it lingered on for years.

> You may be disappointed if you fail,
> but you are doomed if you don't try.
> -*Beverly Sills*

BLOCK NUMBER 24

WASTEFUL TRAINING TO BECOME A VEHICLE-SALESMAN

With this medical area road permanently blocked, CD was again lured into vehicle-sales training. He got invited for an interview by the special trainer who came all the way from Chicago to conduct the course; and my friend was chosen with others to undergo this training that should last for three weeks, at one of the prominent car sales facilities, after which all those who did well would be given automatic employment. As usual, CD's enthusiasm was high as the course progressed, and at the end of which participants were tested and CD was among the successful ones. It was then left for the management to select those who were suitable for their purpose, and unfortunately my friend was not among.

However, hope was not completely lost. This company's other branch agreed to take all those who passed but were not chosen due to vacancy situation, to further participate in their own training course undertaken by another Trainer also from Chicago for another two weeks. They all gladly obliged and after the course, CD was again chosen this time with some other men and a lady to start work immediately. They were all very glad and went through the rigors of preliminary routines at vehicle sales establishments, after the required paper works.

But surprisingly, after just two days, one of them failed to turn up for work. CD did not attach importance to the development, because he thought the man was to report on a later time or on alternate days. But no, he was relieved of his position. As all the new staff were wondering how and why that happened, the immediate supervisor invited CD into his office the morning of the third day, and broke the heart-breaking news to him that his services would not be required after all, as management had found out that more than they needed were employed!

Once again, just as he thought he had managed to be free from that medical **Block**, *Number 24* appeared and made CD run into it head-on; and this situation dealt the final blow on him to stop looking for any more employment in that city for the rest of his stay there. The annoying thing about this whole course is that all were asked to pay for the certificates, which fact was not revealed to them at the beginning until after the course was completed. The meaning of this ***Block Number 24*** is that CD found himself in yet another money wasting venture in another futile job-searching attempt. Yet he still remained smiling.

> When written in Chinese, the word crisis
> is composed of two characters.
> One represents danger and the
> other represents opportunity.
> -John F. Kennedy

IRONY OF FATE VS SUCCESS STORY

**Reasons Why One
Should Remain Smiling**

Now it is time to see the following few successes of CD as opposed to the irony of fate that befell some of his advisers, friends, competitors, and detractors which go to confirm all the quotations about perseverance, determination, and faith in God in one's life struggle.

CD – A Qualified Stenographer

It turned out that my friend not only went successfully trough the ordeal of shorthand-writing training and passed all the required tests to attain the top position in office that it qualifies him for. The irony is that not only the guy who discouraged CD from taking a course to improve himself was in reverse the person who, with all the English he claimed to have known more than CD, being a high-school graduate, failed to pass shorthand test to qualify for Stenographer position.

> The great pleasure in life is
> doing what people say you cannot do.
> -*Walter Bagehot*

❖❖❖

CD – Successfully completed his Foreign Service

Agreeing with the saying that "Man is the architect of his own fortune", CD followed his mind, and in spite of many stumbling blocks, achieved success in his chosen career. In the end, my friend got vindicated when he later saw and heard what went wrong with all those his hitherto competitors; friends; and other so-called well-wishers; and advisers, who on several occasions tried to dissuade him from fighting through all those blocks.

Ironically, it was some of CD's adviser-friends who could not wade through the ordeals in the Foreign Service; not because their stories were all wrong, but because they chose other methods of survival while in there. As already known, the apartheid aspect of the condition of labor was real; and CD in addition, discovered the beast-of-burden nature of the Confidential Secretary's duties at post. Yet, already having a mind-set, my friend refused to be swayed otherwise. Instead, he remained determined to use the opportunity to improve himself. This resolve eventually paid off for CD; while his advisers fell by different way sides. Following is just a brief glimpse of these fellows' fall out of the Foreign Services.

♣ Amadabọ

First, Amadabọ was the elder friend who discouraged CD from venturing into shorthand writing. but ironically as stated earlier, after failing to achieve success in his shorthand writing training, he remained as ordinary Clerical Officer, and later got promoted to the rank of an Executive Officer.

Under that category, Amadabọ got his first and only diplomatic posting to a European country. But that posting was cut short when he ran into trouble with his boss, the Ambassador, over a fight for the heart of a female locally employed lady. The report of that Ambassador against CD's adviser was so bad that he was not only called back home, but also abruptly retired from service!

◆◆◆

♣ Ìlọmabọ

Second, among the Executive Officer-Advisers, Ìlọmabọ, got too clever by trying to cheat the system. After losing his first wife, he kicked off a relationship with a fellow female Executive officer, and both eventually got married, but kept it secret to the Ministry. So, when Ìlọmabọ first went on posting abroad, he maneuvered through his "long-leg" to get his female partner also posted to the same Mission.

There had always been married couples in the Ministry. But the rule is that either of them could get posted individually; and if the partner wanted to join his/her other half he/she was allowed to do so, but without separate allowance, as the one on posting would get his/her allowance at "married rate", while the one that joined the partner would be granted leave of absence with only home salary. But this Ìlọmabọ and his wife tried to be smart by receiving allowances individually though married and living together in one apartment.

Things went on fine for a long time but eventually the bubble got busted, as they were discovered and both recalled home and dismissed from Service!

♦♦♦

♣ Okoloba

The third Executive Officer, Okoloba, got posted to the Americas; but for some unknown reasons, his stay was cut short and he was asked to return home prematurely. Such premature recalls are not new, but Okoloba could not just succumb to such unprepared recall. So, instead of complying with the return order, he vacated his official quarters and disappeared into thin air.

Sadly enough, since life would not just be easy to manage under such situation in a far-away land with no immediate means of sustainable livelihood, he later ended up taking his own life, leaving behind his stranded family!

♦♦♦

♣ Mangi

In the case of the three Confidential Secretaries, the first, Mangi, also absconded into thin air in one of the American cities also, trying to escape arrest for embezzling his country's students' scholarship money. This had no connection whatsoever with his work and entitlements at post. It was purely criminal in nature. Although as part of his jack-of-all-trade responsibilities, he was put in charge of looking after students on government scholarships; which allowed money sent to these students pass through him. But instead of handing over the checks to the entitled students as they arrived, the guy would cash some for his personal use and keep on deceiving the affected students that their money had not arrived.

But on the D-Day nemesis caught up with him when he went to cash a particular check. The clerk at the bank suspected something wrong with that check submitted, and went behind the counter with it for consultation. The unusually long consultation became unbearable for Mangi, and he decided to abscond. He guessed right indeed, because the bank officials behind the counter were alerting the Police of that illegal transaction; and when the corps eventually arrived, Mangi had disappeared. Being such a smart guy, he neither went back to the office, nor returned home to his wife and kids; thus, abandoning his diplomatic carrier and family in a foreign land!

Mangi's community eventually took up the responsibility of repatriating the wife and kids back home as his disappearing act seemed permanent. However, after several years doing menial jobs and taxi-driving still in that city, Immigration officials got hold of him, and repatriated him with no chance to salvage any of his belongings!

♦♦♦

♣ Nimitẹin

The second Confidential Secretary, Nimitẹin, could not hold on any longer than his first posting, putting in his letter of voluntary retirement soon as he landed back home from his second posting. He was reacting to a local job offer by what appeared out of the blues, and mistook it for God-sent opportunity to get rid of this "good-for-nothing" Foreign Service. Initially he seemed happy but by the time situation at this local office showed him signs that condition there would not be better than where he was running away from, it was too late.

Eventually, Nimitẹin was booted out from that establishment for being too headstrong. Meanwhile, before he got to that stage, his wife of so many years had abandoned him for leaving the diplomatic service against her advice. After leaving that local establishment, Nimitẹin became so helpless and spent the rest of his life in perpetual want, and remained in a sorry state.

♦♦♦

♣ Opu-Ḍa

The third Confidential Secretary, Opu-Ḍa, managed to stay it out, but could not make any head-way until he was forced to leave office. As this compulsory retirement recall was broken to him at post, it posed great predicament for him that he also refused to return home to retire. After over-staying the scheduled date to report at Headquarters, and having been already retired from service, he was ordered out of his official quarters, and his pay and all allowances stopped.

Opu-Ḍa then became a refugee in his erstwhile diplomatic country – moving his belongings to a shared apartment with a private compatriot! To worsen the sad story, just after a little time past, thieves (most probably in secret connivance with his compatriot host) invaded that apartment, and carted away as much of his valuables as they could gather; forcing him to prematurely return home to resort to begging from his erstwhile co-staffers.

♦♦♦

Indeed, these friends who discouraged CD from getting into the Foreign Service, were the first to leave the place in questionable circumstances, while my friend maintained his steadfast determination to endure these many heavy burdens and remained smiling even more!

CD – A PACE-SETTER

Coming back to my friend; it is worth knowing that ever before the above successes, CD had set the most surprising first ever in his native traditional music field. As was already presented above, my friend was a renowned traditional drummer, playing clay-pot for singing groups and dancing women; as well as other drum music for men's masquerade societies. He spent more than twenty years of his life - from childhood to adulthood - in this profession.

Playing music generally attracts fame and pleasure; especially for clay-pot drummers who are well-known and popular among the female sex. This situation pushes many drummers to go with the wind and drop woefully after the wind stops blowing. Moreover, clay-pot drummers in particular, were generally looked down upon by other men, with the belief that their regular and close association with the female sex defiles and make them less sanctified than the ordinary Kalabari man! For this reason, many people never expected CD to advance beyond that local level.

But CD surprised them all, and refused to stay down on that level in life. Though he was a celebrity in the entire community of his country's fourth largest tribe; yet, he decided to call it quits; becoming the one and only traditional drummer of that category able to move out to become a success story in modern life.

> Eventually we will find (mostly in retrospect, of course)
> that we can be very grateful to those people
> who have made life most difficult for us.
> - *Ayya Khema*

CD – A United Nation's Diplomat

After retiring from his country's Foreign Service that refused to accord him the title, CD immediately got employed by the United Nations Organization in New York City as a diplomat. The amazing discovery he made was that at this world body, which is the custodian of international diplomacy, all employees, irrespective of their job and status, are diplomats while abroad; and they all carry the same green-colored passport. Moreover, while on official travels only the Secretary-General and his deputies fly first class; but notably, all other UN diplomats fly business class! In his country's diplomatic duties he flew economic class, just as all other staff, except Ambassadors.

Moreover, in terms of remuneration, monthly salaries at the UN are based on their official ranks only at Headquarters; and while at post, their Foreign Service allowance remains the same, irrespective of their ranks. As diplomats, they all have diplomatic immunity and protection; and are all equally entitled to shop at stores designated for diplomats.

My friend thus served his term out as a United Nations Field Officer; retiring with full acquired benefits and gratuities – an amount that makes what he got from his over twenty-five years' service in his country's Civil Service, pales so disgracefully!

Have patience and wait for the divine decree.
Do not become like the foolish laborer
who is removed from the king's palace
for demanding his wages ahead of time.
-Sheikh Abdul Qadir Jillani

STUMBLING BLOCKS - BLESSINGS IN DISGUISE

I do not know what CD is up to next, but almost passing through life in very similar circumstances like him, I found the truism that God will not hear and open His door for you if you continue to knock at the wrong spot that looks like a door. The saying that: "when one door closes, another opens", proved very true in CD's case when at the end of what looked like his last stumbling block, he utilized the time forced on him to remain home, to write and finalize his manuscripts, which were published in quick succession. So, CD remained very grateful to the Almighty for all the blocks he *encountered* and put behind.

This book – Stumbling Blocks – is published in honor of CD's success, as well as an inspiration to young fellows, not to regard stumbling blocks as brick walls, but instead stepping stones. In a Kalabarị adage, mother-roach advised her kids against being afraid, and running out of the bed-frame being flushed with hot water to get rid of their infestation. Mama-Bedbug's reasoning is that anyone that endures the heat will survive; but all other escapees will surely face imminent death under the broom of the waiting bed-owner.

> Be patient. Whatever that is hot,
> will soon get cold.

Now, we know that indeed, stumbling blocks are blessing in disguise in the life of humans. The fatalist believes in destiny and so surrenders himself to events as they happen to him. But the idealist believes that man is the architect of his own destiny. The more I grow older, the more I see proofs that stumbling blocks are really blessings in disguise; because many life events turn out right for me in the end. Believe you me; not becoming what I aspired to be was indeed a blessing in disguise, and that smiling in the face of difficulties is not misplaced after all.

> *Shoot for the moon. Even if you miss it,*
> *you will land among the stars.*
> *- Les Brown*

THE LESSON LEARNED

The summary lesson of this story is that my best friend CD, born to be a Fisherman; barely able to afford the modest rent for one tiny room in some very poor, multi-family abode in one of the slums of the big city, fought hard to improve himself and eventually turned out to be a success story. That was a man many thought the chances of a celebrated life were very slim, if not non-existent. That assessment is not far-fetched, as quite a hand-full of friends who grew in the same category could not go beyond that stage. However, like the proverbial sphinx, CD's eyes were open, and avenues unfolded for him to improve his lot further. My friend was able to further his education abroad, and migrated to the States. No doubt, the stint in life abroad also afforded him and his family the wherewithal to take care of their life, and settle their children.

As we learned from the story of the donkey, life is bound to shovel all kinds of dirt on you; and the trick to getting out of the well is to shake it off and take a step up. Each of our troubles is a steppingstone. We can get out of the deepest wells just by not stopping, and never giving up. Shake it off and take a step up one by one! This has been the doctrine that keep CD remain smiling in the face of life-long series of **stumbling Blocks!**

SONNY O. BRAIDE

Live in the world like a waterfowl;
the water clings to the bird,
but the bird shakes it off.
Live in the world like a mudfish;
the fish lives in the mud,
but its skin is always bright and shiny.
- Ramakrishna (Hindu Wisdom)

THE ROAD TO SUCCESS

My friend's younger children had no inkling, nor could they want to believe what he passed through to reach the stage they came to see him in. Poor kids, no one can blame their ignorance, or should I say innocence. They were luckily born with silver spoon in the mouth. CD was born with no spoon at all in his mouth; but with so much resilience, struggling and deprivation, I am sure my friend will want to give them, and other humans – young and old - this guide to the road to success:

On the road to success there is:

- a curve called - FAILURE;
- a loop called - CONFUSION
- speed bumps called - FRIENDS
- red lights called – ENEMIES; and
- caution lights called – FAMILY; as well as
- flats called - JOBS.

But if one has:

- a spare called - DETERMINATION
- an engine called - PERSEVERANCE
- an insurance called - FAITH; and
- a Driver called GOD,

One will make it to a place called - SUCCESS!

This all means that what is really needed in life to succeed is resilience and hard work. Action eradicates fear. To do anything worthwhile in the world we must not stand back shivering and thinking of the cold and danger; but jump in and scramble through; because to get what you have never had, you must do what you have never done. That's why I believe, CD agreed with all these great humans for coming up with such encouraging and inspiring sayings and quotations in this book.

Twenty years from now you will be more disappointed by the things you did not do than by the ones you did do.

BE GRATEFUL TO GOD IN ALL CIRCUMSTANCES

We, humans must always praise God as much for a closed door as He gives an open one. The reason God closes doors is because He has not prepared any worthy thing over there for us. If He did not close the wrong door, we would never find the right door. God directs our path through the closing and opening of doors. When one door closes, it forces us to change our course; and when another door closes, it forces us to change our course again. This will go on until finally, we find the open door and just walk right into our blessing.

Really, the Lord directs our paths through the opening and closing of doors, but instead of praising Him for the closed door (which keeps us out of trouble), we get upset because we judge by appearances. For God, there is neither yesterday nor tomorrow. Everything to Him is **NOW**! And because He walks ahead of us, He can spot trouble down the road and set up a *Roadblock or Detour* accordingly. But through our lack of wisdom, we try to tear down the roadblocks; or push aside the detour sign. Then the minute we get into trouble, we start crying "Lord how could You have allowed this to happen?!

I am very much like CD, who is so grateful for the many stumbling blocks that come seemingly never ending in my way. Indeed, my life experience has confirmed that frowning not only put heavy strain on the facial muscles, but also dampens the human aura. Smiling frightens away the devil and opens a private pipeline to the music of Angels which promotes good health, longer life and above all, perpetual happiness. Indeed, different experiences present different painful results that can send less fortitude people do things they later regret. But that is the point – **fortitude**. The important point is to make stepping-stones out of stumbling blocks that come one's way.

Nevertheless, as beauty is in the eyes of the beholder, so also is success in the eyes of its possessor. That means one can become super rich and yet remain unfulfilled. That is unfortunate. Like CD, I was born poor, but with smile on my face; and what reinforced my belief to stay in that mood all through life's never-ending ***Stumbling Blocks*** is this philosophy by Deng Ming-Dao, a Chinese Philosopher which says:

"The journey of humanity is the journey from ignorance
to enlightenment. It's an endless march of souls through eternity.
If you are standing in an infinitely long line of souls, how can you say
that your position is superior or inferior to others?
When there is no head and no end to the line,
it doesn't matter what place you hold."

> I thank God for my handicaps -
> for, through them, I have found
> myself, my work, and my God.
> *- Helen Keller*

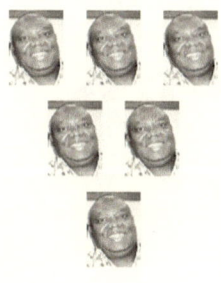

ACKNOWLEGEMENT

God gave you a gift of 86,400 seconds today.
Have you used one to say "thank you"?
-*William A. Ward*

I thank the Almighty, for seeing me through so many blocks; as well as delivering me from dangers – many of them unseen.

I cannot list all the people who made it possible for this book. But my sincere gratitude goes to my unknown detractors and ill-wishers; especially those who made life difficult for me. Their action pushed me to fight harder to achieve more progress; thus, disappointing their evil expectations.

I am so very grateful to be blessed with Godly children; especially my First Daughter – Deaconess Debra Braide-Abili, and my first Granddaughter – Apostle Princess Belemzy – of Belemzy Ministries, who single-handedly sponsored the publication of this book. Remain blessed, my God-given daughters; and continue to fulfill your heavenly duties to humanity.

QUOTATIONS USED IN THIS BOOK

My great thanks and appreciation go to those inspired authors, whose apt quotations used in this book, formed the bedrock of my success story in life through many stumbling blocks.

1. If there's a book you really want to read, but it hasn't been written yet, then you must write it. *-Toni Morrison*
2. --cursed is the ground for your sake. In sorrow shall you eat of it all the days of your life. Thorns also and thistles shall it bring forth unto you-- In the sweat of your face shall you eat bread till you return unto the ground *-Gen. 3: 17-19.*
3. The fairest graciousness, they say, is a kindly look. Wherever it thrives, the whole world flourishes. *- Hindu Wisdom*
4. God gave you a gift of 86,400 seconds today. Have you used one to say "thank you"? *-William A. Ward*
5. Life is ten percent what happens to you, and ninety percent how you respond to it. *-Lou Holtz*
6. If the Moon is your friend, you'll never work in darkness. *-Ghanaian Saying*
7. If you find a path with no obstacles, it probably doesn't lead anywhere. *-Frank A. Clark*
8. Over every mountain there is a path, although it may not be seen from the valley. *-James Rogers*

9. Obstacles don't have to stop you. If you run into a wall, don't turn around and give up. Figure out how to climb it, go through it, or work around it. -*Michael Jordan*
10. When someone tells me there is only one way to do things, it always lights a fire under my butt. My instant reaction is, "I'm going to prove you wrong! -*Picabo Street*
11. It is better to be prepared for an opportunity and not have one than to have an opportunity and not be prepared. - *Whitney Young, Jr.*
12. When we fall on the ground it hurts us, but we also need to rely on the ground to get back up. -*Kathleen McDonald*
13. Determination gives you the resolve to keep going despite the road-blocks that lay before you. -*Denis Waitley*
14. There is always room at the top" as Daniel Webster said, when advised against being a lawyer: "There is always room at the top. - *Daniel Webster*
15. If you fail to prepare, you're prepared to fail. - *Mark Spitz*
16. You cannot prevent the birds of sorrow from flying over your head; but you can prevent them from building nests in your hair. -*Chinese Proverb*
17. f you want to see the sun shine, you have to weather the storm. - *Frank Lane*
18. The elevator to success is out of order. You'll have to use the stairs - one step at a time. -*Joe Girard*
19. Do not pray for easy lives. Pray to be stronger men. Do not pray for tasks equal to your powers. Pray for powers equal to your tasks. - *Phillips Brooks*
20. You never will be the person you can be if pressure, tension, and discipline are taken out of your life. -*James, G. Bilkey*
21. There never was night that had no morn. -*Dinah Maria Mulock Craik*

22. I will read and improve myself; for one day, I know my time will come. -*Abraham Lincoln*
23. There is no greater dignity than that of the man who declares, 'I will never cease in laboring to advance my family.' Perseverance and sound understanding - these two are what exalt a man's family. When a man declares he will advance his family, God Himself will wrap His robes and lead the way. - *Hindu principle*
24. Out of difficulties grow miracles. -*Jean de la BruyFe*
25. If you see ten troubles coming down the road, you can be sure that nine will run into the ditch before they reach you. -*Calvin Coolidge*
26. When it is dark enough, you can see the stars. -*Charles A. Beard*
27. We can complain that rose bushes have thorns; or we can rejoice that thorn bushes have roses. - *Abraham Lincoln*
28. My imperfections and failures are as much a blessing from God as my successes and my talent; and I lay them both at His feet. -*Mohandas Gandhi*
29. What I aspired to be and was not, comforts me. -*Robert Browning*
30. Losers see thunderstorms, Winners see rainbows. Losers see icy streets, Winners put on their ice skates! - *Denis Waitley*
31. You may be disappointed if you fail, but you are doomed if you don't try. -*Beverly Sills*
32. When written in Chinese, the word crisis is composed of two characters. One represents danger and the other represents opportunity. -*John F. Kennedy*
33. The great pleasure in life is doing what people say you cannot do. -*Walter Bagehot*
34. Eventually we will find (mostly in retrospect, of course) that we can be very grateful to those people who have made life most difficult for us. - *Ayya Khema*

35. Have patience and wait for the divine decree. Do not become like the foolish laborer who is removed from the king's palace for demanding his wages ahead of time. -*Sheikh Abdul Qadir Jillani*
36. Shoot for the moon. Even if you miss it, you will land among the stars. -*Les Brown*
37. Live in the world like a waterfowl; the water clings to the bird, but the bird shakes it off. Live in the world like a mudfish; the fish lives in the mud, but its skin is always bright and shiny. -*Ramakrishna (Hindu Wisdom)*
38. The journey of humanity is the journey from ignorance to enlightenment. It's an endless march of souls through eternity. If you are standing in an infinitely long line of souls, how can you say that your position is superior or inferior to others? When there is no head and no end to the line, it doesn't matter what place you hold. - *Deng Ming-Dao*
39. God gave you a gift of 86,400 seconds today. Have you used one to say "thank you? -*William A. Ward*
40. I thank God for my handicaps - for, through them, I have found myself, my work, and my God. -*Helen Keller*
41. Mother Roach warns kids: "Be patient. Whatever that is hot, will soon get cold." -*Kalabari adage*

OTHER BOOK TITLES BY THE AUTHOR

1. Celebrating the dead in Kalabarị

A story based in his native culture of the Kalabarị people in Rivers State, Nigeria. It chronicled how people die; and how dead bodies are treated according to the manner of death. This includes celebrating elaborately those who merit it, and discarding of the cadaver of those who die under despicable circumstances.

2. Testimony Of God's Many Miracles In My Life

Testimony is the documentation of the numerous events in which God systematically and steadfastly intervened in the writer's life. These interventions, coming miraculously at all times, include: saving him from imminent dangers; providing sustenance where no known means of livelihood existed; diverting his course to avert imminent harm or demise; and above all, giving him healthy life, spanning over seventy years.

The book is Mr. Braide's show of utter gratefulness to the Almighty for His grace, steadfast, and miraculous intercessions in his struggles through life. It is his hope and prayer that the book will prepare people's minds to experience God's miracles as well; knowing that the Great One cares for all in just the same way He cared for Mr. Braide in similar circumstances.

3. Owuamẹ Kẹngẹma Kalaḅarị

Owuamẹ Kẹngẹma Kalaḅarị is a history, culture, and traditional story of the great Kalaḅarị people. As a history book, it tries to present stories and events as they happened without fear or favor; devoid of any attempt to degrade anyone or glorify others.
Reinforced with the importation of religions from outside – Christianity and Islam - and the bombardment of the population by their propagandists, mainly for monetary gains, the average Kalaḅarị citizen had for long been at a loss as to if he/she ever had any real culture; and if there were, could these cultural activities be all evil, wrong and must be discarded?! For this reason, even those few who would have liked to know a thing or two about their culture, have no chance or opportunity to benefit from it for lack of available information materials.

There had earlier been a few stories here and there written by expatriates who had had contacts with the people; but their honest and unbiased endeavors were not as whole as they should be. Only of late, other interested indigenes' attempts to produce books intended to carry valuable materials about the Kalaḅarị people have heavily come short, as such endeavors lack lots of basic facts and accuracy. Not too surprisingly, some of these stories tend to lean towards sectionalism that pays encomiums to some factions and factional personalities; as well as belittling others.

In the case of traditional performing arts, boys who indulge in it at tender age, and have the positive inclination to understand the drum language, abandon the idea as soon as they leave school and get employed in paid jobs outside the community. This is why CD decided to take up the gauntlet to keep this authentic culture alive in print not only for those who might want to use it for performing sake, but also as a source of information for all interested to know all about the great Kalaḇarị people.

www.ingramcontent.com/pod-product-compliance
Lightning Source LLC
Chambersburg PA
CBHW021428070526
44577CB00001B/107